OXFORD PICTURE DICTIONARY

Content Areas for Kids

Jenni Currie Santamaria
Joan Ross Keyes

Program Consultant
Kate Kinsella

OXFORD
UNIVERSITY PRESS

OXFORD
UNIVERSITY PRESS

198 Madison Avenue
New York, NY 10016 USA

Great Clarendon Street, Oxford, OX2 6DP, United Kingdom

Oxford University Press is a department of the University of Oxford.
It furthers the University's objective of excellence in research, scholarship,
and education by publishing worldwide. Oxford is a registered trade
mark of Oxford University Press in the UK and in certain other countries

First published in 2012

1 2 3 4 5 6 7 8 9 10   17 16 15 14 13 12

Library of Congress Cataloging-in-Publication Data

Oxford picture dictionary content areas for kids : accelerates academic
language development / [edited by] Jenni Currie Santamaria, Joan Ross
Keyes ; program consultant: Kate Kinsella. – 2nd ed.
    p. cm.
 1. English language–Dictionaries, Juvenile. 2. Picture dictionaries,
English–Juvenile literature. 3. Interdisciplinary approach in
education. I. Santamaria, Jenni Currie. II. Keyes, Joan Ross. III.
Kinsella, Kate.
  PE1628.5.O97 2011
  423'.17–dc23
                2011036091

General Manager, American ELT: Laura Pearson
Publisher: Stephanie Karras
Managing Editor: Marni Sabin
Associate Editor: Charlotte Roh
Director, ADP: Susan Sanguily
Executive Design Manager: Maj-Britt Hagsted
Designer: Sangeeta E. Ramcharan
Electronic Production Manager: Julie Armstrong
Production Artist: Elissa Santos
Image Manager: Trisha Masterson
Senior Image Editor: Fran Newman
Senior Manufacturing Controller: Eve Wong

ISBN: 978 0 19 401775 6

Printed in China

This book is printed on paper from certified and well-managed sources

ACKNOWLEDGEMENTS

Illustrations by: Scott Angle: 110-111, 144-145; Lalena Fisher: 32 (bot.), 33 (top),
54 (bot.), 55 (top), 80 (bot.), 81 (top), 90(bot.), 91 (top), 104 (bot.), 105 (top), 124
(bot.), 125 (top), 128-129, 136 (bot.), 137 (top), 154 (bot.), 155 (top), 158-159, 168
(bot.), 169 (top); Ken Gamage: 7; Leslie Harrington: 12-13, 14-15, 16-17, 18-19,
20-21, 22-23, 24-25, 26-27, 28-29, 30-31, 34-35, 36-37, 38-39, 40-41, 42-43, 44-45,
46-47, 164-165; Nathan Jarvis: 78-79, 88-89, 138-139, 146-147, 152-153, 156-157;
John Kaufmann: 140-141, 148-149; Shawn McKelvey: 56-57, 60-61, 62-63, 68-69,
70-71, 82-83, 108-109, 130-131, 132-133, 142-143; Jorge Santillan: 6, 8-9, 10-11,
48-49, 50-51, 52-53, 150-151; Scott Seibel: 58-59, 72-73, 74-75; Ben Shannon:
64-65, 66-67, 76-77, 84-85, 86-87, 92-93, 94-95, 96-97, 98-99, 100-101, 102-103,
106-107, 112-113, 126-127, 134-135, 160-161, 162-163, 166-167; Sam Tomasello:
114-115, 116-117, 118-119, 120-121, 122-123; Sam Ward: 5;
Back cover: Shortkut/shutterstock.com (laptop).

Cover Illustrator: Leslie Harrington
Cover Design: Molly K. Scanlon

Acknowledgments

Series Consultant

Kate Kinsella, Ed.D., has a rich and varied background teaching youth and writing curricula to support their English language and literacy growth. She completed her doctorate in second language acquisition and multicultural education at the University of San Francisco, where she accepted a faculty position in San Francisco State University's Center for Teacher Efficacy. A highly sought after teacher educator and program advisor, she provides training and consultancy nationally to state departments, districts, and individual schools. She stays actively involved teaching English Learners across the K–12 grade levels, providing in-class lesson demonstrations and coaching. A former TESOL Fulbright scholar, Dr. Kinsella has served as the editor of the CATESOL Journal and as the chief K–12 editor on the TESOL Journal. Dr. Kinsella has also served as the pedagogical guide for numerous English learner programs and dictionaries, including the *Oxford Picture Dictionary for the Content Areas.* She plans to dedicate the next decade of her professional life to creating engaging, relevant curricula that enables teachers to advance English language and literacy for immigrant youths so they exit secondary school both college and career ready.

Assessment Expert

Margo Gottlieb, Ph.D., is a national expert in the design of assessments for English Language Learners, in the evaluation of language education programs, and in the development of English language proficiency standards in pre-K–12 settings. Currently, she is Director of Assessment and Evaluation for the Illinois Resource Center and Lead Developer for the World-Class Instructional Design and Assessment (WIDA) Consortium at the Wisconsin Center for Education Research at the University of Wisconsin. Margo has a Ph.D. in Public Policy Analysis, Evaluation Research and Program Design, an M.A. in Applied Linguistics, and a B.A. in the teaching of Spanish. She has published an extensive array of materials, including monographs, handbooks, books, and a dozen book chapters.

Authors

Jenni Currie Santamaria holds an MFA in TEFL/ESL and has been working with English learners of various ages and levels since 1989. She has served as an ESL instructor, technology mentor, curriculum developer, and teacher trainer. Her publications include numerous interactive materials and teaching guides, including the lesson plans for the *Oxford Picture Dictionary*.

Joan Ross Keyes is a former ESL teacher with more than 20 years of classroom experience in both elementary and junior high schools. Joan has facilitated ESL workshops around the country and was also an adjunct professor at Long Island University for many years. Her passion for teaching English learners contributed to the success of the original *Oxford Picture Dictionary for Kids*.

National Standards and Content Area Consultants

Social Studies Expert

Jeff Passe, Ph.D., is Chair of the Department of Secondary Education at Towson University in Maryland. He specializes in curriculum and social studies. A former elementary school teacher, he is the author of five books and dozens of chapters and articles. His research primarily focuses on the teaching of current events. In 2008, he completed his term on the Board of Directors of the National Council for the Social Studies, highlighted by his presidency from 2005–2006.

Science Expert

Julie A. Luft, Ph.D., is a Professor of Science Education at Arizona State University at Tempe, Fulton Graduate School of Education, and Research Director for the National Science Teachers Association. She has been the professional investigator of several professional development and research grants. Dr. Luft has served as president and board member of the Association for Science Teacher Education, on the Board of the National Science Teachers Association, and she has been Associate Editor for several journals.

Math Expert

Vena M. Long, Ed.D., is a Professor of Mathematics Education and Associate Dean for Research and Professional Development at the University of Tennessee. Dr. Long served on the Board of Directors of the National Council of Teachers of Mathematics from 2006–2010 and is also active in local- and state-level professional organizations.

Our Advisory Committee

English Learner Expert

Linda New Levine, Ph.D., is a consultant with the Center for Applied Linguistics. She advises teachers of English language learning children and programs for teaching English as a Foreign Language in both primary and secondary classrooms. She has been a teacher of English as a Second Language in K–12 classrooms and a Staff Development Facilitator for the Bedford Central School district in New York. She was also an adjunct assistant professor of ESL Methods and Materials at Teachers College, Columbia University.

Literacy Expert

Charlene Cobb, Ed.D., is Executive Director for Teaching and Learning in East Maine School District 63 in Des Plaines, Illinois. Over the past twenty years she has worked nationally with schools and districts to support literacy programs as a teacher, reading specialist, professor, consultant, and an advocate across all domains of content. She is particularly interested in the literacy development of linguistically diverse learners and struggling readers, and believes that building background knowledge through the development of academic vocabulary is critical to closing the achievement gap.

Special Education Expert

Donnalyn Jaque-Anton is an educational consultant working with schools and districts on the integration of general and special education and response to intervention and instruction to ensure academic achievement for all students. She brings years of practical experience as a teacher at all levels, a principal, and as a district administrator. As the former Executive Officer of Los Angeles Unified School District (LAUSD), she implemented a visionary plan for students with disabilities (Schools for All Children) which erased the culture of failure for that group of "at risk" students in the nation's second largest school district.

The publisher and author would like to acknowledge the following individuals for their invaluable feedback during the development of this program.

Sandra Garnett: Albany County School District #1, WY

Patricia Milazzo: Alief ISD, TX

Ronald DeFalco: Bellwood District 88, IL

Linda Camerino: Bladen County Schools, NC

Mary E. Kaiser: Blaine County School District, ID

Kathryn Mizuno: Camden City School District, NJ

Catherine Fox: Central Falls School District, RI

Lisa Marie Lewis, Siobhan Lavin Mulvey: Charlotte-Mecklenburg Schools, NC

Griselda E. Flores: Chicago Public Schools, IL

Blaire Brandon, Jessica Maston: Clayton County Public Schools, GA

Camelia Courtright, Vicki Sue Steenhoek: Cobb County School District, GA

Sarah Rowan: Copiague UFSD, NY

Klodia Ibrahim: Dearborn Public Schools, MI

Nancy Foskey: DeKalb County School System, GA

Diann Mackey: Des Moines Public Schools, IA

Mary Beth Scott: Downingtown Area School District, PA

Catherine Spencer: East Allen County Schools, IN

Katherine Zlogar: East Maine District 63, IL

Pam Garvie: Enid Public Schools, OK

Huong Banh: Evanston/Skokie District 65, IL

Doris Cook, Nancy Ellen Cook: Fort Worth ISD, TX

Jennifer Sijmons: Greenwich Public Schools, CT

Felicia Bundy: Guilford County Public Schools, NC

Johanna McPhee: Hampton School District, NH

Gail Cogdill: Harnett County Schools, NC

Patsy Mills: Houston ISD, TX

Esmeralda Polanco: Irving ISD, TX

Charlotte Johnson: Lebanon School District, NH

Stacy Rowan: Lewisville ISD, TX

Amy S. Cochran: Metropolitan Nashville Public Schools, TN

Roslyn Eisner, Janet E. Lasky, Ann E. Morgan: Montgomery County Public Schools, MD

Amy Irene Halsall: MSD Warren Township, IN

Lisa Allphin, Joan Doyle: Mt. Diablo USD, CA

Lisa Spencer: Newark Central School District, NY

Misty Campos: Orange USD, CA

Eunice Alvarado-Martinez, Tamara Lopez, Enrique Rivera-Torres, Carmen S. Santiago: Orange County Public Schools, FL

Rita Tantillo: Paradise Valley USD, AZ

Maureen Carmody, Alison Garcia: Patchogue-Medford UFSD, NY

Mary E. McConville: Pittsford School District, NY

Beth Anderson: Plano ISD, TX

Lisa Rinehart: Plano CUSD 88, IL

Edie Thompson: Purdy R-II School District, MO

Patricia Lewno: Racine USD, WI

Anna R. Ferro: Rochester City School District, NY

Fiona Lyons: Rye Neck School District, NY

Kristine B. Heim: Saint Paul Public Schools, MN

Eileen Marchetti: Shenandoah Valley School District, PA

Sarah Steele: Warsaw Community Schools, IN

Anne Hagerman Wilcox: Wendell School District, ID

Mèlanie R. Álvarez: White Plains Public Schools, NY

Letter to Students

Hello! My name is Dr. Kate Kinsella. I'm a professor who helps many people become excellent teachers. I helped with this amazing picture dictionary. I know it will help you learn many useful new words.

My own son, John Carlos, is an English learner like you! He was born in Guatemala and he speaks Spanish. He loves looking at the beautiful and exciting pictures. At home, he likes to play "I Spy" with his sister, Jane Dzung, to find new words in the big picture. At school, he has fun working with a partner to practice using the new words.

At first, some words may seem difficult. Don't worry! I know if you say, read, and write the words often, you will become a terrific English speaker just like my son. I believe in you!

All my best,

Dr. Kate

How to Use this Dictionary

Topic Pages

These pages teach you new words with a big picture. You will look at the big picture, read new words, and have interesting things to talk about.

This box tells you the topic number.

This box tells you the topic name.

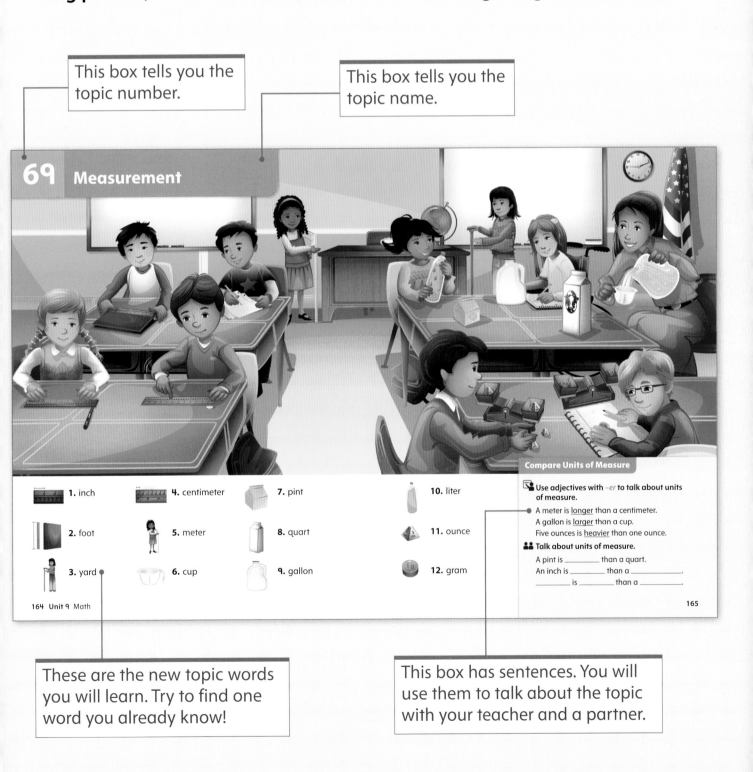

69 Measurement

1. inch
2. foot
3. yard
4. centimeter
5. meter
6. cup
7. pint
8. quart
9. gallon
10. liter
11. ounce
12. gram

Compare Units of Measure

Use adjectives with *-er* to talk about units of measure.

- A meter is <u>longer</u> than a centimeter.
- A gallon is <u>larger</u> than a cup.
- Five ounces is <u>heavier</u> than one ounce.

Talk about units of measure.

A pint is _____ than a quart.
An inch is _____ than a _____.
_____ is _____ than a _____.

164 Unit 9 Math

165

These are the new topic words you will learn. Try to find one word you already know!

This box has sentences. You will use them to talk about the topic with your teacher and a partner.

Unit Opening Pages

These pages are at the beginning of each unit. They have useful words that you will need in school, at home, and in your community.

Each word or phrase has a picture to show you what it means.

11 A Day at School

1. read

2. write

7. work with a partner

8. work in a group

3. draw

4. repeat

9. ask questions

10. answer questions

5. think

6. raise hand

Discuss School Activities

Use the verb *does* to ask questions about the students.

A: What <u>does</u> Alex do at school?
B: He reads.

B: What <u>does</u> Jasmine do at school?
A: She works in a group.

A: What <u>does</u> Tyler do at school?
B: He answers questions.

Ask and answer questions about the students at school.

A: What _____ Elena do at school?
B: She writes.

B: What does _____ do at school?
A: _____.

The word in color shows you the language skill that you will learn.

Unit Expansion Pages

These pages are at the end of each unit. Your teacher will help you with activities to use the unit words in new ways.

These are charts. You will use the charts to organize words from the unit.

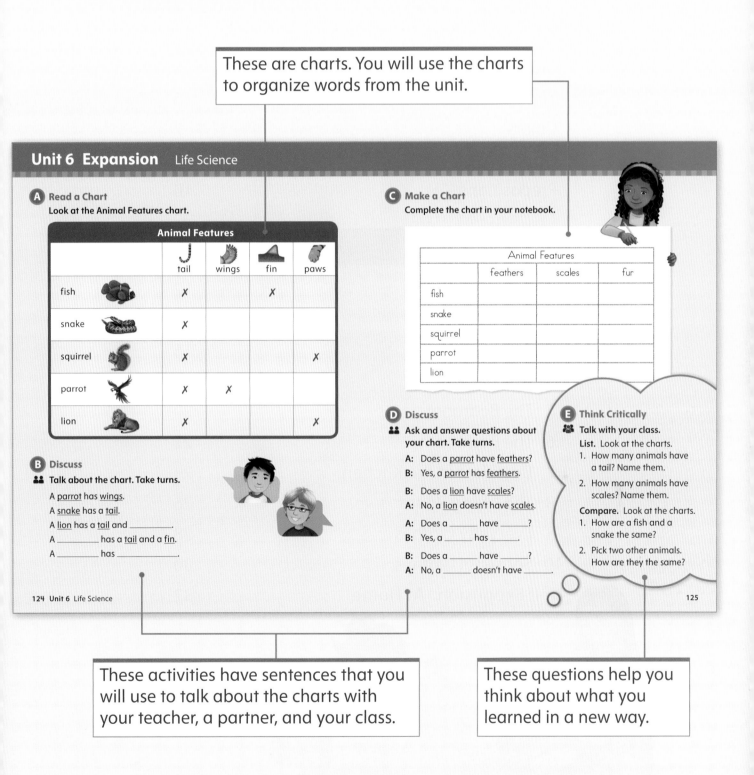

Unit 6 Expansion Life Science

A Read a Chart
Look at the Animal Features chart.

Animal Features		tail	wings	fin	paws
fish		X		X	
snake		X			
squirrel		X			X
parrot		X	X		
lion		X			X

B Discuss
Talk about the chart. Take turns.
A parrot has wings.
A snake has a tail.
A lion has a tail and _____.
A _____ has a tail and a fin.
A _____ has _____.

C Make a Chart
Complete the chart in your notebook.

Animal Features			
	feathers	scales	fur
fish			
snake			
squirrel			
parrot			
lion			

D Discuss
Ask and answer questions about your chart. Take turns.
A: Does a parrot have feathers?
B: Yes, a parrot has feathers.

B: Does a lion have scales?
A: No, a lion doesn't have scales.

A: Does a _____ have _____?
B: Yes, a _____ has _____.

B: Does a _____ have _____?
A: No, a _____ doesn't have _____.

E Think Critically
Talk with your class.
List. Look at the charts.
1. How many animals have a tail? Name them.
2. How many animals have scales? Name them.

Compare. Look at the charts.
1. How are a fish and a snake the same?
2. Pick two other animals. How are they the same?

These activities have sentences that you will use to talk about the charts with your teacher, a partner, and your class.

These questions help you think about what you learned in a new way.

Table of Contents

Unit 2 At School

Unit 3 Community

Unit 4 The United States

Unit 5 Health

Unit 6   Life Science

Unit 7   Physical Science

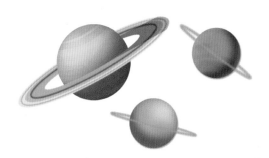

Unit 8   Earth and Space Science

Unit 9   Math

Meet the Kids

Alex

Elena

Jasmine

Tyler

Getting Started

Numbers

1	one	●
2	two	● ●
3	three	● ● ●
4	four	● ● ● ●
5	five	● ● ● ● ●
6	six	● ● ● ● ● ●
7	seven	● ● ● ● ● ● ●
8	eight	● ● ● ● ● ● ● ●
9	nine	● ● ● ● ● ● ● ● ●
10	ten	● ● ● ● ● ● ● ● ● ●
11	eleven	● ● ● ● ● ● ● ● ● ● ●
12	twelve	● ● ● ● ● ● ● ● ● ● ● ●
13	thirteen	● ● ● ● ● ● ● ● ● ● ● ● ●
14	fourteen	● ● ● ● ● ● ● ● ● ● ● ● ● ●
15	fifteen	● ● ● ● ● ● ● ● ● ● ● ● ● ● ●
16	sixteen	● ● ● ● ● ● ● ● ● ● ● ● ● ● ● ●
17	seventeen	● ● ● ● ● ● ● ● ● ● ● ● ● ● ● ● ●
18	eighteen	● ● ● ● ● ● ● ● ● ● ● ● ● ● ● ● ● ●
19	nineteen	● ● ● ● ● ● ● ● ● ● ● ● ● ● ● ● ● ● ●
20	twenty	● ● ● ● ● ● ● ● ● ● ● ● ● ● ● ● ● ● ● ●

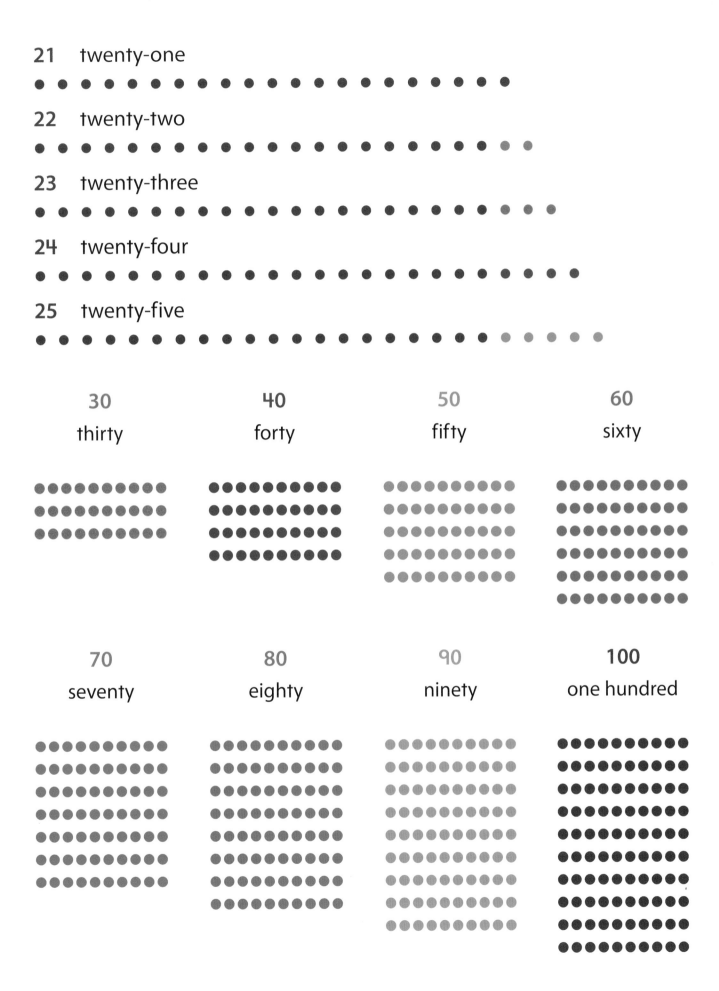

21 twenty-one

22 twenty-two

23 twenty-three

24 twenty-four

25 twenty-five

| **30** | **40** | **50** | **60** |
| thirty | forty | fifty | sixty |

| **70** | **80** | **90** | **100** |
| seventy | eighty | ninety | one hundred |

Ordinal Numbers

1st first	★	☆	☆	☆	☆	☆	☆	☆	☆	☆
2nd second	☆	★	☆	☆	☆	☆	☆	☆	☆	☆
3rd third	☆	☆	★	☆	☆	☆	☆	☆	☆	☆
4th fourth	☆	☆	☆	★	☆	☆	☆	☆	☆	☆
5th fifth	☆	☆	☆	☆	★	☆	☆	☆	☆	☆
6th sixth	☆	☆	☆	☆	☆	★	☆	☆	☆	☆
7th seventh	☆	☆	☆	☆	☆	☆	★	☆	☆	☆
8th eighth	☆	☆	☆	☆	☆	☆	☆	★	☆	☆
9th ninth	☆	☆	☆	☆	☆	☆	☆	☆	★	☆
10th tenth	☆	☆	☆	☆	☆	☆	☆	☆	☆	★

Calendar

Days of the Week

Sunday	Monday	Tuesday	Wednesday	Thursday	Friday	Saturday
		1	2	3	4	5
6	7	8	9	10	11	12
13	14	15	16	17	18	19

Months of the Year

January

1	2	3	4	5	6	7
8	9	10	11	12	13	14
15	16	17	18	19	20	21
22	23	24	25	26	27	28
29	30	31				

February

					1	2	3	4
5	6	7	8	9	10	11		
12	13	14	15	16	17	18		
19	20	21	22	23	24	25		
26	27	28	29					

March

			1	2	3
4	5	6	7	8	9	10
11	12	13	14	15	16	17
18	19	20	21	22	23	24
25	26	27	28	29	30	31

April

1	2	3	4	5	6	7
8	9	10	11	12	13	14
15	16	17	18	19	20	21
22	23	24	25	26	27	28
29	30					

May

	1	2	3	4	5
6	7	8	9	10	11	12
13	14	15	16	17	18	19
20	21	22	23	24	25	26
27	28	29	30	31		

June

					1	2
3	4	5	6	7	8	9
10	11	12	13	14	15	16
17	18	19	20	21	22	23
24	25	26	27	28	29	30

July

1	2	3	4	5	6	7
8	9	10	11	12	13	14
15	16	17	18	19	20	21
22	23	24	25	26	27	28
29	30	31				

August

		1	2	3	4
5	6	7	8	9	10	11
12	13	14	15	16	17	18
19	20	21	22	23	24	25
26	27	28	29	30	31	

September

						1
2	3	4	5	6	7	8
9	10	11	12	13	14	15
16	17	18	19	20	21	22
23	24	25	26	27	28	29
30						

October

	1	2	3	4	5	6
7	8	9	10	11	12	13
14	15	16	17	18	19	20
21	22	23	24	25	26	27
28	29	30	31			

November

				1	2	3
4	5	6	7	8	9	10
11	12	13	14	15	16	17
18	19	20	21	22	23	24
25	26	27	28	29	30	

December

						1
2	3	4	5	6	7	8
9	10	11	12	13	14	15
16	17	18	19	20	21	22
23	24	25	26	27	28	29
30	31					

Time

morning

night

afternoon

evening

noon

midnight

Colors

red   orange   yellow   green

blue   purple   pink   tan

brown   black   white   gray

Opposites

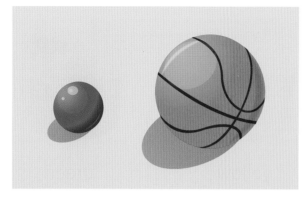

small   large

left   right

new   old

open   closed

short   tall

slow   fast

full   empty

light   heavy

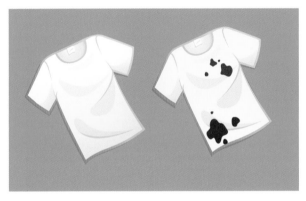

clean   dirty

wet   dry

cold   hot

same   different

Prepositions

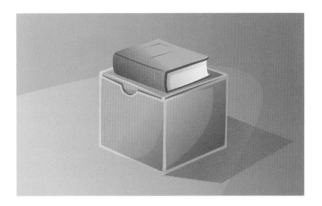

The book is **on** the box.

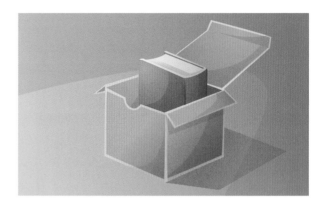

The book is **in** the box.

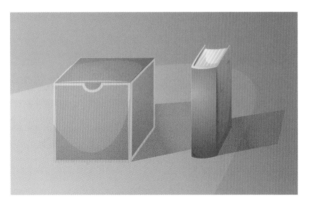

The book is **next to** the box.

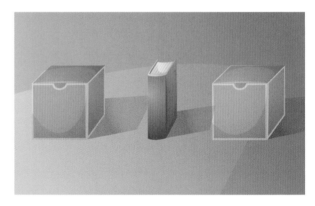

The book is **between** the boxes.

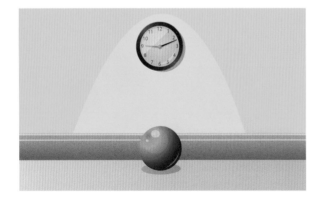

The clock is **above** the ball.
The ball is **below** the clock.

The girls are **in front of** the boys.
The boys are **behind** the girls.

The girl is **across from** the boy.

The ball goes **through** the hoop.

The boy goes **up** the stairs.

The girl goes **down** the stairs.

The girl goes **around** the tree.

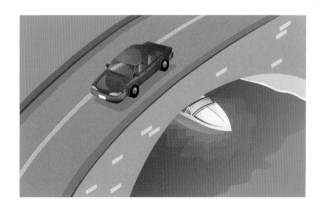

The car goes **over** the bridge.
The boat goes **under** the bridge.

1 Every Day

1. wake up

2. take a shower

3. take a bath

4. get dressed

5. comb hair

6. eat breakfast

7. eat dinner

8. do homework

9. brush teeth

10. go to bed

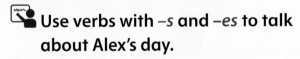

Discuss Daily Activities

Use verbs with –s and –es to talk about Alex's day.

He <u>wakes</u> up at 7:00 a.m.
He <u>gets</u> dressed at 7:30 a.m.

He <u>does</u> homework at 7:00 p.m.
He <u>goes</u> to bed at 8:15 p.m.

Talk about Alex's day.

comb hair

He ~~~~s his hair at 7:40 a.m.
He _____es his teeth at 8:00 p.m.

He _____ breakfast at _____.
He _____ at _____.

2 Friends

Tyler

Alex

 1. eyes

 4. hair

 7. long

 2. eyelashes

 5. bangs

 8. short

 3. glasses

 6. ponytail

 9. straight

Jasmine

Elena

Describe People

10. curly

11. dark

12. light

Use the verb *has* to talk about people.

Alex <u>has</u> bangs.

Jasmine <u>has</u> dark hair.

Talk about the friends.

Elena _____ a ponytail.

Tyler _____ glasses.

She has _____.

He has _____.

15

3 Family

Clara

Patti

Elena

Rosa

David

Angela

Alan

 1. sister

 4. father

 7. grandfather

 2. brother

 5. parents

 8. grandparents

 3. mother

 6. grandmother

 9. great-grandmother

Martin

Tony

Eva

Angie

Daniel

Identify Family Relationships

 10. aunt

 11. uncle

 12. cousin

Use the verbs *is* and *are* to talk about family.

Patti <u>is</u> her sister.

Angie and Daniel <u>are</u> her cousins.

Talk about Elena's family.

Tony _____ her uncle.

David and Rosa _____ her grandparents.

_____ is her _____.

_____ are her _____.

17

4 Home

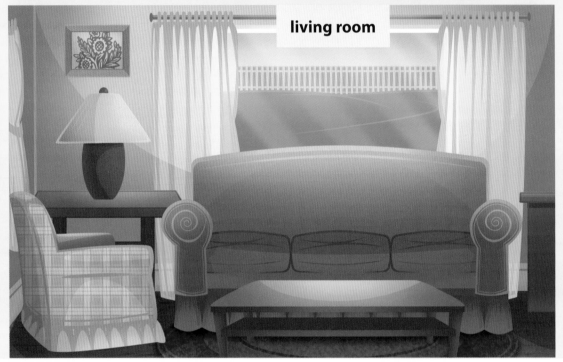

living room

 1. sink

 4. mirror

 7. wall

 2. door

 5. picture

 8. stairs

 3. lamp

 6. window

 9. table

bathroom

bedroom

kitchen

Discuss Things in the Home

10. floor

11. eat

12. cook

Use *There is* _____. and *There are* _____. to talk about things in the home.

<u>There is</u> one window.

<u>There are</u> two sinks.

<u>There are</u> three lamps.

Talk about the things in the home.

There is one _____.

There are two _____.

There is _____.

There are _____.

19

5 The Bedroom

 1. bed

 2. blanket

 3. pillow

 4. closet

 5. dresser

 6. desk

 7. drawer

 8. alarm clock

 9. toys

10. puzzle

11. pick up

12. put away

Describe Location

 Use the prepositions *in, on,* **and** *under* **to talk about where things are.**

The toy is <u>in</u> the drawer.
The alarm clock is <u>on</u> the desk.
The puzzle is <u>under</u> the dresser.

Talk about where things are in the bedroom.

The _____ is in the _____.
The _____ is on the _____.
The _____ is under the _____.
The _____ is _____ the _____.

21

6 The Bathroom

 1. water

 2. bathtub

 3. toilet

 4. shampoo

 5. soap

 6. towel

 7. toothbrush

 8. toothpaste

 9. comb

Discuss Things People Use

10. brush

11. wash

12. dry

📝 **Use the preposition *with* to talk about things people use.**

She washes her face <u>with</u> soap.
He brushes his teeth <u>with</u> a toothbrush.
She dries her hands <u>with</u> a towel.

👥 **Talk about the things people use in the bathroom.**

He washes his hair _____ shampoo.
She combs her hair _____ a comb.
He _____ with _____.
She _____ with _____.

23

7 Breakfast in the Kitchen

 1. stove

 4. counter

 7. eggs

 2. refrigerator

 5. cup

 8. grapes

 3. cabinet

 6. plate

 9. bananas

10. butter

11. bread

12. cereal

Determine Location

Use *Where is* _____? and *Where are* _____? to ask about location.

A: <u>Where is</u> the bread?
B: It's on the counter.

B: <u>Where are</u> the plates?
A: They're on the table.

Ask and answer questions about where things are in the kitchen.

A: Where _____?
B: _____.

25

8 The Living Room

 1. sofa

 2. rug

 3. television

 4. remote

 5. radio

 6. music

 7. telephone

 8. listen

 9. talk

Describe Actions at Home

10. play

11. study

12. help

Use verbs with *–ing* to talk about what people are doing.

He's <u>listening</u> to music.

She's <u>studying</u>.

They're <u>playing</u> a game.

Talk about what people are doing in the living room.

He's _____ing on the phone.

She's _____ing _____.

He's _____ing _____.

Nd

9 Everyday Clothes

 1. dress

 2. skirt

 3. pants

 4. jeans

 5. T-shirt

 6. sweatshirt

 7. pajamas

 8. underwear

 9. socks

10. cap

11. shoes

12. sneakers

Determine Clothing Colors

Use *What color is _____?* and *What color are _____?* to ask about colors.

A: <u>What color is</u> the T-shirt?

B: It's purple.

B: <u>What color are</u> the jeans?

A: They're blue.

Ask and answer questions about colors.

A: What color _____?

B: _____.

29

Winter Holidays

Rainy Spring

 1. sweater

 2. hat

 3. scarf

 4. gloves

 5. boots

 6. umbrella

 7. raincoat

 8. shorts

 9. sunglasses

Summer Vacation

Windy Fall

Describe People's Clothes

10. bathing suit

11. sandals

12. jacket

Use the verb *wearing* to talk about people's clothes.

He's <u>wearing</u> a raincoat.
She's <u>wearing</u> a sweater.
They're <u>wearing</u> hats.

No

Talk about the people in the pictures.

He's wearing _____.
She's wearing _____.
They're wearing _____.

A Read a Chart

Look at the Things at Home chart.

Things at Home		kitchen	living room	bedroom	bathroom
sofa			X		
sink		X		X	X
refrigerator		X			
bed				X	X
window		X	X	X	X

B Discuss

Talk about the chart. Take turns.

There is a <u>sink</u> in the <u>bathroom</u>.

There is a <u>sofa</u> in the <u>living room</u>.

There is a <u>bed</u> and a _____ in the <u>bedroom</u>.

There is a _____ and a <u>refrigerator</u> in the _____.

There is a _____ in the _____.

C Make a Chart

Complete the chart in your notebook.

Things at Home	kitchen	living room	bedroom	bathroom
table		sofos		
dresser				
shower				
stove				
mirror				

D Discuss

Ask and answer questions about your chart. Take turns.

A: Is there a <u>stove</u> in the <u>kitchen</u>?

B: Yes, there is a <u>stove</u> in the <u>kitchen</u>.

B: Is there a <u>table</u> in the <u>bathroom</u>?

A: No, there isn't a <u>table</u> in the <u>bathroom</u>.

A: Is there a _____ in the _____?

B: Yes, there is _____.

B: Is there a _____ in the _____?

A: No, there isn't _____.

E Think Critically

Talk with your class.

List. Look at the charts.

1. How many rooms have a window? Name them.

2. How many things are in the kitchen? Name them.

Compare. Look at the charts.

1. Which things are in the bedroom and living room?

2. Pick two other rooms. Which things are in both rooms?

11 A Day at School

1. read

2. write

3. draw

4. repeat

5. think

6. raise hand

7. work with a partner

8. work in a group

What is this?

9. ask questions

This is an apple.

10. answer questions

Discuss School Activities

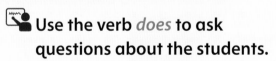 **Use the verb *does* to ask questions about the students.**

> **A:** What <u>does</u> Alex do at school?
> **B:** He reads.
>
> **B:** What <u>does</u> Jasmine do at school?
> **A:** She works in a group.
>
> **A:** What <u>does</u> Tyler do at school?
> **B:** He answers questions.

Ask and answer questions about the students at school.

> **A:** What _____ Elena do at school?
> **B:** She writes.
>
> **B:** What does _____ do at school?
> **A:** _____.

12 The School

classroom

office

 1. crossing guard

 2. bus driver

 3. student

 4. principal

 5. teacher

 6. teacher's aide

 7. librarian

 8. secretary

 9. nurse

library

computer room

art room

music room

nurse's office

cafeteria

restroom

gym

Locate People at School

10. cafeteria worker

11. custodian

12. coach

Use *Where is _____?* to ask about people at school.

A: <u>Where is</u> the teacher?

B: She's in the classroom.

B: <u>Where is</u> the custodian?

A: He's in the restroom.

Ask and answer questions about where people are.

A: Where is the _____?

B: _____'s in the _____.

37

13 School Supplies

 1. pencil

 2. colored pencil

 3. pencil sharpener

 4. eraser

5. pen

 6. crayon

 7. marker

8. scissors

 9. calculator

Indicate Possession

10. book

11. binder

12. backpack

Use *have* and *has* to talk about school supplies.

He <u>has</u> an eraser.

She <u>has</u> two pens.

They <u>have</u> colored pencils.

Talk about what the students have.

She has _____.

He has _____.

They have _____.

14 The Classroom

 1. paper

 2. notebook

 3. glue

 4. tape

 5. ruler

 6. chair

 7. trash can

 8. board

 9. clock

Read your book.
Write your...

Describe Location

Use the prepositions *on* or *in* to talk about where things are.

The globe is <u>on</u> the desk.
The clock is <u>on</u> the wall.
The notebook is <u>in</u> the desk.
The paper is <u>in</u> the trash can.

Talk about where things are in the classroom.

The map is _____ the wall.
The paper is _____ the desk.
The _____ is _____ the _____.

 10. globe

 11. map

 12. flag

41

15 The Library

 1. catalog

 2. call number

 3. dictionary

 4. atlas

 5. newspaper

 6. magazine

 7. DVD

 8. bookshelves

 9. library card

Describe Actions at the Library

10. check out

11. return

12. look

Use verbs with *–ing* to talk about what someone is doing.

He's <u>checking</u> out a book.

She's <u>returning</u> a DVD.

They're <u>looking</u> at the catalog.

Talk about what the students are doing in the library.

He's _____ing _____.

She's _____ing _____.

They're _____ing _____.

16 The Computer Lab

 1. computer

 4. mouse

 7. printer

 2. monitor

 5. headphones

 8. Internet

 3. keyboard

 6. microphone

 9. cursor

NO FOOD OR DRINK

10. log in

11. type

12. click

Describe Actions in the Lab

Talk about what students are doing in the computer lab with the verb *using*.

She's <u>using</u> a microphone.

He's <u>using</u> a mouse.

They're <u>using</u> computers.

Talk about what students are using in the computer lab.

He's using _____.

She's using _____.

They're using _____.

45

 1. tray

 2. bottle

 3. bag

 4. carton

 5. can

 6. sandwich

 7. salad

 8. strawberries

 9. carrots

Describe Containers of Food

10. crackers

11. juice

12. milk

Use the preposition *of* to talk about food in the cafeteria.

She has a bag <u>of</u> carrots.

He has a can <u>of</u> juice.

She has a carton <u>of</u> milk.

Talk about lunch in the cafeteria.

She has a bag _____ crackers.

He has a bowl _____ strawberries.

She has a _____ of _____.

He has a _____ of _____.

18 Physical Education

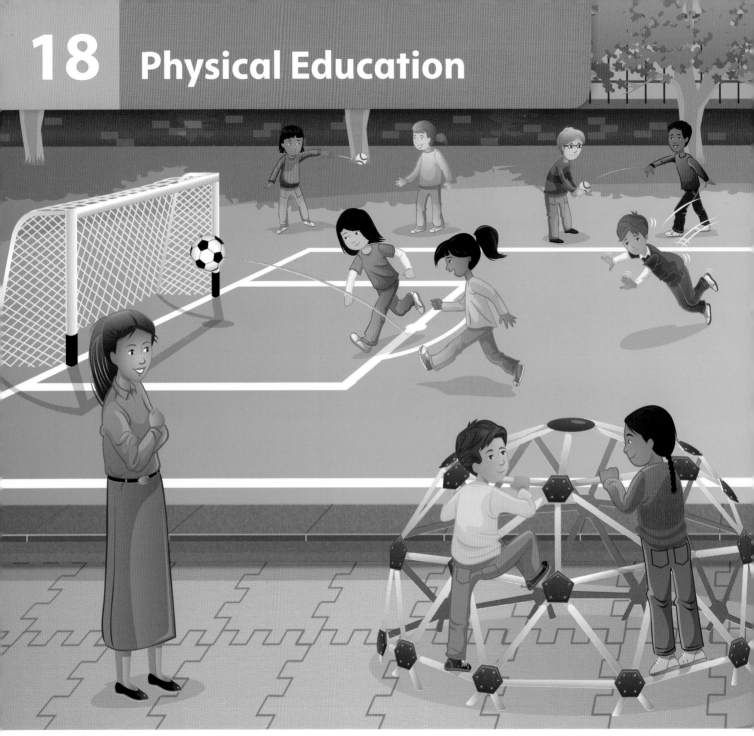

 1. field

 2. court

 3. basket

 4. balls

 5. jump

 6. bounce

 7. throw

 8. catch

 9. kick

Describe Physical Actions

10. run

11. fall

12. climb

 Use action verbs **to talk about what people are doing.**

He <u>throws</u> the ball.

She <u>kicks</u> the ball.

He <u>bounces</u> the ball on the court.

Talk about what the students are doing.

He _____ the ball.

She _____ on the field.

He _____.

She _____.

 1. earache

 2. fever

 3. sore throat

 4. cut

 5. stomachache

 6. thermometer

 7. tissues

 8. bandage

 9. bleed

Discuss Health

10. cough

11. sneeze

12. lie down

Use *What's the matter with _____?* to ask about someone's health.

A: <u>What's the matter with</u> him?
B: He has an earache.

B: <u>What's the matter with</u> her?
A: She's lying down.

Ask and answer questions about the students.

A: _____ with _____?
B: _____.

51

 1. tired

 2. sad

 3. happy

 4. surprised

 5. angry

 6. scared

 7. confused

 8. smile

 9. frown

10. yawn

11. cry

12. laugh

Describe Feelings

Use adjectives to talk about people's feelings.

Jasmine feels <u>angry</u>. She's frowning.
The boy feels <u>tired</u>. He's yawning.
The girl feels <u>happy</u>. She's smiling.

Talk about how the students feel.

Tyler feels _____. He's laughing.
Elena feels _____. She's frowning.
The boy feels _____. He's _____.
The girl feels _____. She's _____.

A Read a Diagram

Look at the Venn diagram.

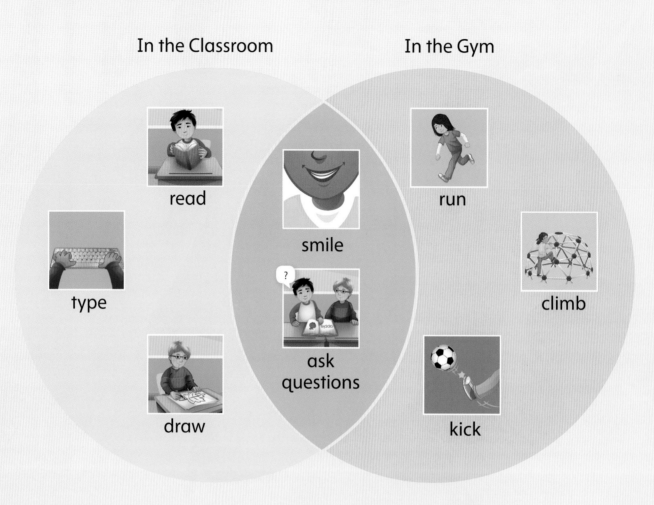

In the Classroom

In the Gym

read

type

draw

smile

ask questions

run

climb

kick

B Discuss

Talk about the diagram. Take turns.

Students <u>read</u> in the classroom.

Students <u>run</u> in the gym.

Students <u>smile</u> in the classroom and the gym.

Students _____ in the _____.

Students _____ in the _____ and the _____.

C Make a Diagram

Complete the Venn diagram in your notebook.

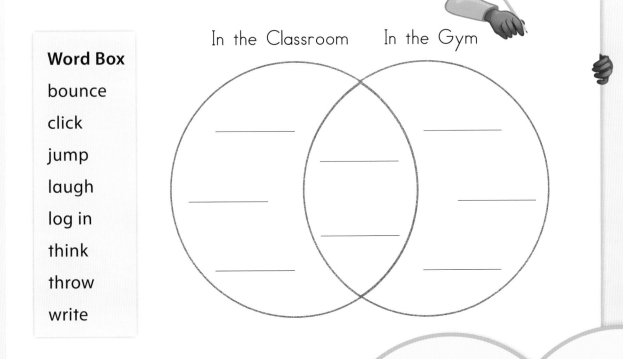

Word Box

bounce

click

jump

laugh

log in

think

throw

write

In the Classroom   In the Gym

D Discuss

👥 **Ask and answer questions about your diagram. Take turns.**

A: Do students <u>jump</u> in the gym?

B: Yes, they <u>jump</u> in the gym.

B: Do students <u>write</u> in the gym?

A: No, they don't <u>write</u> in the gym.

A: Do students think in the _____?

B: Yes, _____.

B: Do students _____?

A: _____, they _____.

E Think Critically

👥 **Talk with your class.**

List. Look at the diagrams.

1. What do students do in the classroom?

2. What do students do in the classroom and the gym?

Make Connections. Look at the diagrams.

1. What do you do in the classroom? In the gym?

2. What else do you do at school?

1. build houses

2. fix cars

3. sell clothing

4. deliver mail

5. serve food

6. take care of people

7. protect the community

8. fight fires

9. grow crops

10. raise animals

Discuss People at Work

Use **verbs** to ask and answer questions about what people do at work.

A: What does he <u>build</u>?
B: He <u>builds</u> houses.

B: What does she <u>protect</u>?
A: She <u>protects</u> the community.

A: What does she <u>fix</u>?
B: She <u>fixes</u> cars.

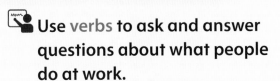 Ask and answer questions about what people do at work.

A: Who does he take care of?
B: He takes care of _____.

B: What does she grow?
A: She _____ crops.

A: What does he _____?
B: He _____.

B: What does she _____?
A: She _____.

57

 1. house

 4. street sign

 7. corner

 2. apartment building

 5. address

 8. streetlight

 3. street

 6. sidewalk

 9. stop sign

Describe Location

10. fence

11. park

12. bench

Use *There's* _____. to talk about places in the neighborhood.

<u>There's</u> a red house on Oak Street.
<u>There's</u> a street sign on the corner.
<u>There's</u> a bench in the park.

Talk about places in the neighborhood.

There's a _____ on the sidewalk.
There's a _____ on Maple Street.
There's _____.

59

 1. police officer

 2. mail carrier

 3. post office

 4. police station

 5. movie theater

 6. museum

 7. intersection

 8. crosswalk

 9. traffic light

Discuss Location

10. mailbox

11. taxi

12. cross the street

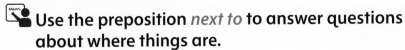

Use the preposition *next to* to answer questions about where things are.

A: Where's the police station?

B: It's <u>next to</u> the movie theater.

Ask and answer questions about where things are in the community.

A: Where's the movie theater?

B: It's _____ the museum.

B: Where's the _____?

A: It's _____.

61

24 Businesses in Town

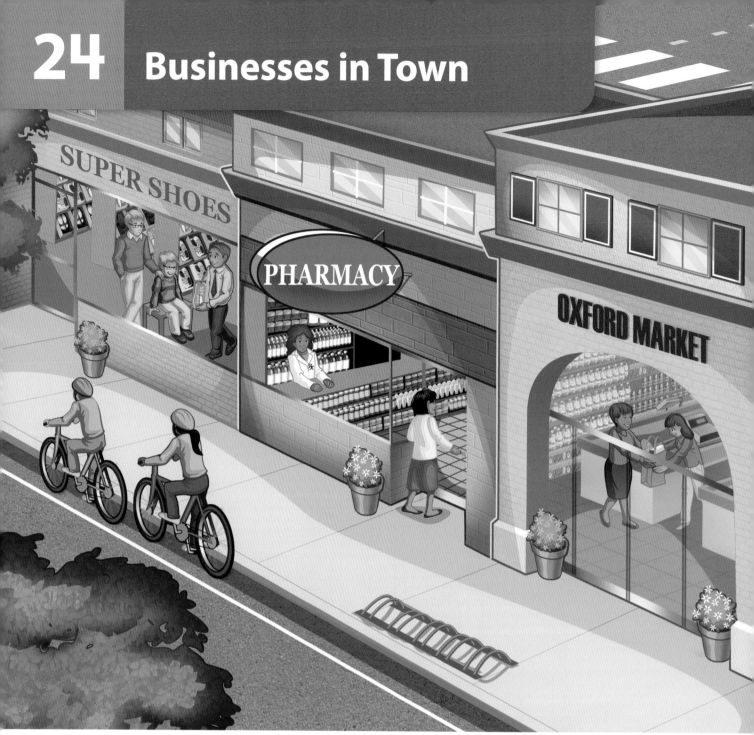

SUPER SHOES

PHARMACY

OXFORD MARKET

 1. cashier

 4. teller

 7. drugstore

 2. pharmacist

 5. customer

 8. shoe store

 3. salesperson

 6. supermarket

 9. bank

LAUNDRY

GAS

GAS

OXFORD MARKET

BANK

SALE

SALE

Discuss Where People Work

10. gas station

11. laundry

12. groceries

Use *Where does* _____ *work?* to ask about people and their jobs.

A: <u>Where does</u> a teller <u>work</u>?

B: A teller works at a bank.

Ask and answer questions about where people work.

A: Where does a pharmacist _____?

B: A _____ works at a _____.

B: Where does a _____ work?

A: A _____ works at a _____.

63

SEAFOOD

MEAT

 1. celery

 4. avocado

 7. orange

 2. lettuce

 5. apple

 8. lemon

 3. tomato

 6. pineapple

 9. list

10. paper towels

11. box

12. cart

Describe Future Actions

Use *going to* to talk about the future.

She's <u>going to</u> buy a lemon.

He's <u>going to</u> buy apples.

They're <u>going to</u> buy paper towels.

Talk about what people are going to buy.

He's _____ buy _____.

She's _____ buy _____.

They're _____ buy _____.

26 The Restaurant

 1. menu

 4. chicken

 7. fork

 2. server

 5. rice

 8. spoon

 3. soup

 6. broccoli

 9. knife

Identify What People Need

 10. napkin

 11. bowl

 12. order

 Use the verb *need* to talk about things that people are missing.

She <u>needs</u> a napkin.

He <u>needs</u> a spoon.

She <u>needs</u> rice.

Talk about what people need at the restaurant.

He _____ a bowl.

She _____ a menu.

He needs _____.

She needs _____.

27 The City

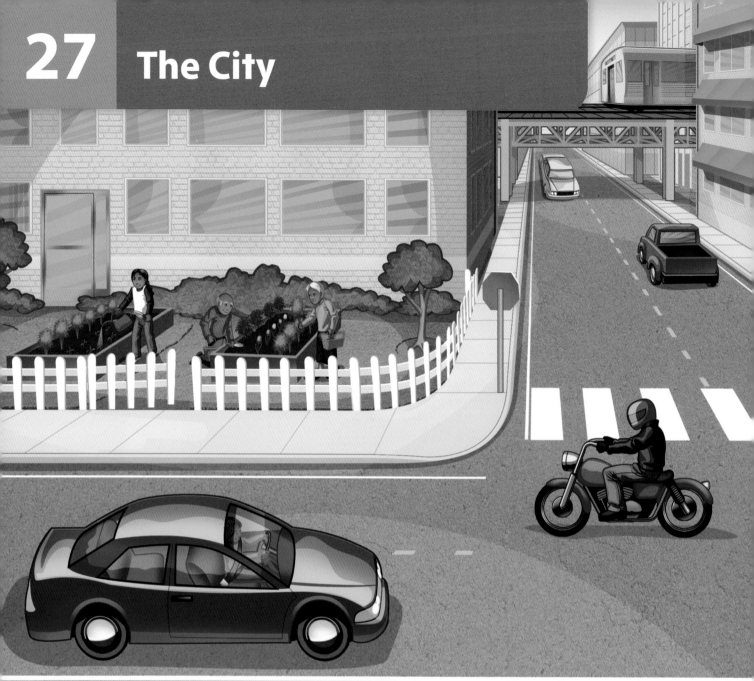

 1. bicycle

 4. bus stop

 7. building

 2. car

 5. seat belt

 8. garden

 3. bus

 6. helmet

 **9.** wait

Describe Transportation

 10. walk

 11. ride

 12. drive

Use **verbs** to talk about getting around the city.

He <u>drives</u> a bus.
She <u>waits</u> for the bus.
They <u>ride</u> bicycles.

Talk about getting around the city.

She _____ a car.
He _____ the bus.
She _____.
He _____.
They _____.

 1. motorcycle

 4. police car

 7. helicopter

 2. truck

 5. train

 8. airport

 3. van

 **6.** airplane

 9. highway

Describe Distance

10. sign

11. factory

12. skyscraper

 Use the prepositions *near* and *far from* to talk about distance.

The helicopter is <u>near</u> the airport.
The factory is <u>far from</u> the train.
The truck is <u>near</u> the motorcycle.

👥 **Talk about the city.**

The _____ is far from the airplane.
The _____ is near the _____.
The _____ is far from the _____.

 1. sailboat

 2. ship

 3. ferry

 4. tugboat

 5. boats

 6. lighthouse

 7. bridge

 8. dock

 9. crane

Identify Quantity

10. life jacket

11. load

12. unload

Use *How many* _____? to ask about the harbor.

A: <u>How many</u> cranes are on the dock?

B: One crane is on the dock.

B: <u>How many</u> cars are on the bridge?

A: Five cars are on the bridge.

Ask and answer questions about the harbor.

A: How many _____ are _____?

B: _____.

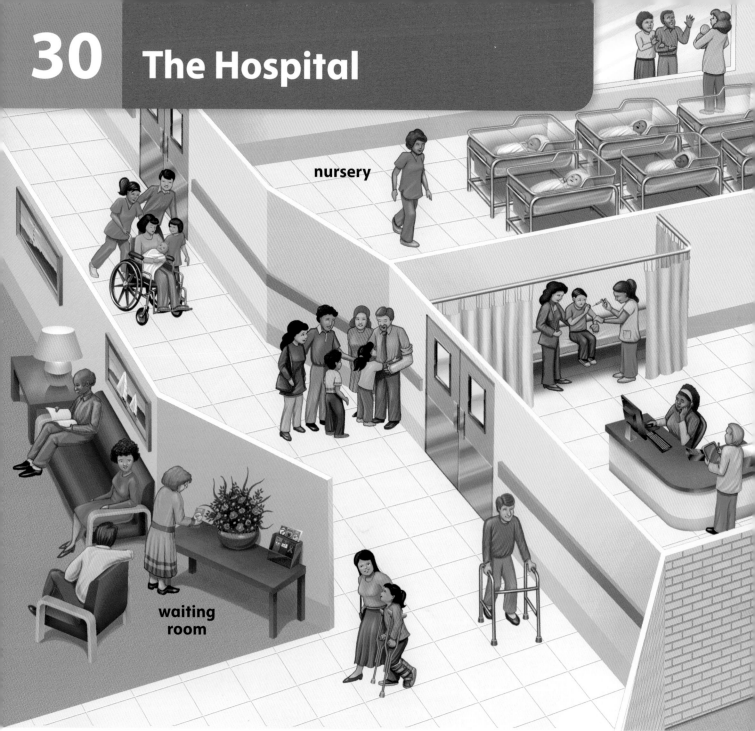

30 The Hospital

nursery

waiting room

 1. wheelchair

 4. shot

 7. paramedic

 2. crutches

 5. X-ray

 8. patient

 3. cast

 6. ambulance

 9. receptionist

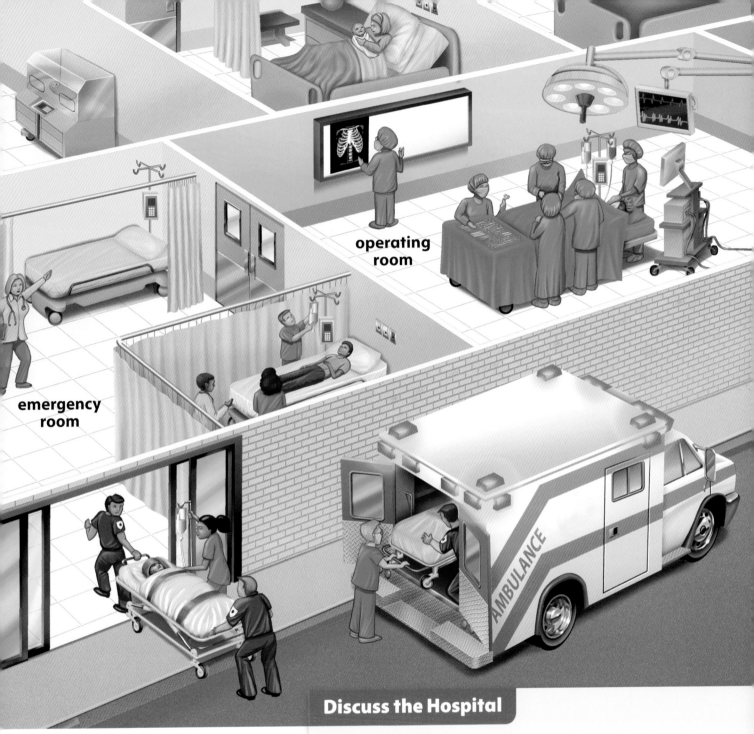

operating room

emergency room

Discuss the Hospital

10. doctor

11. surgeon

12. baby

Use *Who* _____? to ask about people in the hospital.

A: <u>Who</u> is in the emergency room?
B: The receptionist is in the emergency room.

B: <u>Who</u> is in the ambulance?
A: The paramedic is in the ambulance.

Ask and answer questions about people in the hospital.

A: Who is in the _____?
B: The _____ is in the _____.

75

31 Fire Safety

 1. firefighter

 4. matches

 7. battery

 2. uniform

 5. smoke

 8. fire extinguisher

 3. fire truck

 6. smoke detector

 9. fire escape

Don't play with matches!

Does your smoke detector need a battery?

Plan your escape route.

Call 911 for help!

911

Discuss Fire Safety

10. escape route

11. exit

EXIT

12. call 911

Use commands to talk about fire safety.

<u>Know</u> the exits.

<u>Find</u> the fire escape.

<u>Make</u> sure the smoke detector has a battery.

Talk about fire safety.

Don't play with _____.

Call _____ for help.

Plan your escape _____.

Use the _____.

32 The Farm

 **1.** farmer

 4. orchard

 7. chicken

 2. barn

 5. field

 8. cow

 3. tractor

 6. crops

 9. horse

Describe the Farm

10. plow	
11. feed	
12. pick	

 Use verbs to talk about the farm.

She <u>feeds</u> chickens.

The farmer <u>plows</u> the field.

They <u>pick</u> apples in the orchard.

Talk about the farm.

He _____ apples.

She _____ horses in the barn.

They grow crops in the _____.

A Read a Chart

Look at the People and Places chart.

People Who Work →		Places to Work	
police officer		police station	
cashier		supermarket	
mail carrier		post office	
receptionist		hospital	
teller		bank	

B Discuss

 **Talk about the chart. Take turns.**

A <u>police officer</u> works at a <u>police station</u>.

A <u>cashier</u> works at a _____.

A _____ works at a <u>hospital</u>.

A _____ works at a _____.

C Make a Chart

Complete the chart in your notebook.

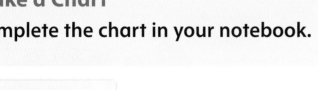

Word Box

doctor
drugstore
farm
farmer
hospital
pharmacist
restaurant
salesperson
server
shoe store

People Who Work ⟶ Places to Work	

D Discuss

👥 **Ask and answer questions about your chart. Take turns.**

A: Who works at a <u>restaurant</u>?

B: A <u>server</u> works at a <u>restaurant</u>.

B: Who works at a <u>drugstore</u>?

A: A _____ works at a <u>drugstore</u>.

A: Who works at a <u>shoe store</u>?

B: A _____ works at a _____.

B: Who works at a _____?

A: A _____ works at a _____.

E Think Critically

👥 **Talk with your class.**

Make Connections. Look at the chart in A.

1. Where does a cashier work?

2. Where else does a cashier work?

Evaluate. Look at both charts.

1. Where do you want to work?

2. Why do you want to work there?

81

33 Biography Verbs

1. be born

2. die

3. explore

4. trade

5. sign a document

6. travel

1880

7. invent

1920

8. immigrate

1976

9. celebrate

Discuss the Past

 Use verbs with *-ed* to talk about the past.

He <u>signed</u> a document in 1776.
She <u>traveled</u> in 1867.
They <u>immigrated</u> in 1920.
They <u>traded</u> in 1770.

👥 **Talk about the past.**

He explored in _____.
She died in _____.
They celebrated in _____.
He _____ in _____.
She _____ in _____.
They _____ in _____.

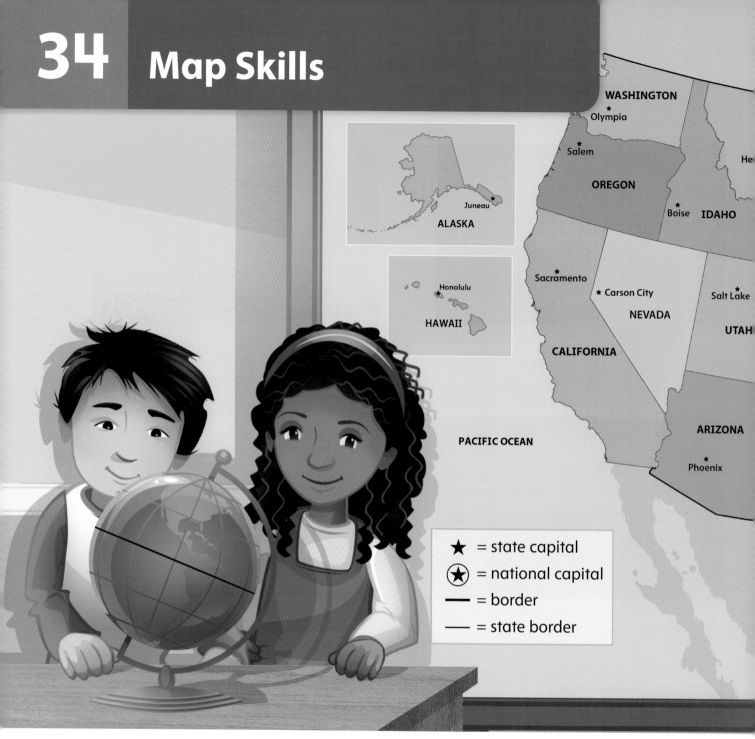

WASHINGTON
★ Olympia

★ Salem

OREGON

He

★ Boise IDAHO

★ Sacramento

★ Carson City

NEVADA

★ Salt Lake

UTAH

CALIFORNIA

PACIFIC OCEAN

ALASKA
★ Juneau

HAWAII
★ Honolulu

ARIZONA

★ Phoenix

★ = state capital
⊛ = national capital
— = border
— = state border

 1. ocean

 2. continent

 3. country

 4. state

 5. capital

 6. border

 7. equator

 8. hemisphere

★ = state capital
⊛ = national capital
— = border
— = state border

9. key

CANADA

MAINE
Augusta

VERMONT
Montpelier

MICHIGAN

NEW HAMPSHIRE
Concord

MASSACHUSETTS
Boston

Albany

RHODE ISLAND
Providence

NEW YORK

CONNECTICUT
Hartford

NTANA

NORTH DAKOTA
★ Bismarck

MINNESOTA

WISCONSIN
★ Madison

St. Paul ★

PENNSYLVANIA
Harrisburg ★

NEW JERSEY
Trenton

SOUTH DAKOTA
Pierre ★

OMING

Lansing ★

MARYLAND
Annapolis

IOWA
★
Des Moines

DELAWARE
Dover

heyenne
★

OHIO

ILLINOIS
★
Springfield

INDIANA
★
Indianapolis

WEST
VIRGINIA

Columbus ★

NEBRASKA

Lincoln ★

Denver ★

WASHINGTON, DC

Richmond ★

MISSOURI

Charleston ★

Frankfort ★

OLORADO

VIRGINIA

Topeka ★

Jefferson City ★

KANSAS

KENTUCKY

Raleigh ★

NORTH CAROLINA

a Fe

Nashville ★

OKLAHOMA
★
Oklahoma City

ARKANSAS
★
Little Rock

TENNESSEE

SOUTH
CAROLINA
Columbia ★

ATLANTIC OCEAN

MEXICO

Atlanta ★

ALABAMA

0   250   500

TEXAS

Montgomery ★

GEORGIA

Miles

Jackson ★

Scale

Austin ★

Baton Rouge ★

Tallahassee ★

MEXICO

LOUISIANA

MISSISSIPPI

FLORIDA

N

W ⊹ E

GULF OF MEXICO

S

Describe a Map

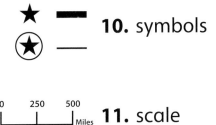

10. symbols

11. scale

N
W ⊹ E
S

12. compass rose

🖥️ **Use the verb *shows* to talk about a map.**

The color blue <u>shows</u> the ocean.
The black line <u>shows</u> the border.
The key <u>shows</u> symbols.

👥 **Talk about the map.**

The star _____ the capital.
The _____ shows the equator.
The _____ shows _____.

85

LEADERS

Country

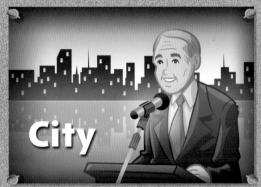

City

State

 1. president

 4. judge

 7. leaders

 2. governor

 5. city council

 8. citizen

 3. mayor

 6. council member

 9. courtroom

City Council Meeting

Court

Election

VOTE HERE

10. speech

11. ballot

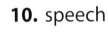

12. vote

Discuss Leaders

Use *Who leads* _____? to ask questions about the government.

A: <u>Who leads</u> the city?

B: The mayor leads the city.

B: <u>Who leads</u> the country?

A: The president leads the country.

Ask and answer questions about the government.

A: Who leads the _____?

B: The _____ leads the _____.

87

Pledge of Allegiance

by Francis Bellamy

I pledge allegiance
to the flag
of the United States
of America,
and to the republic
for which it stands,
one nation under God,
indivisible,
with liberty
and justice for all.

Washington Monument

1. Statue of Liberty

4. Congress

7. memorial

2. White House

5. Supreme Court

8. eagle

3. Capitol

6. monument

9. Pledge of Allegiance

The Star Spangled Banner

by Francis Scott Key
on September 14th, 1814

O! say can you see by the dawn's early light,
What so proudly we hailed at the twilight's last gleaming,
Whose broad stripes and bright stars through the perilous fight,
O'er the ramparts we watched, were so gallantly streaming?
And the rockets' red glare, the bombs bursting in air,
Gave proof through the night that our flag was still there;
O! say does that star-spangled banner yet wave,
O'er the land of the free and the home of the brave?

New York

Lincoln Memorial

Discuss American Symbols

The Star Spangled Banner
by Francis Scott Key
September 14th, 1814

O! say can you see
by the dawn's early light,

10. national anthem

11. stars

12. stripes

Use *What is _____?* to ask questions about American symbols.

A: <u>What is</u> the bald eagle?

B: It's an American symbol.

B: <u>What is</u> "The Star-Spangled Banner"?

A: It's the national anthem.

Ask and answer questions about American symbols.

A: What is _____?

B: It's _____.

89

Unit 4 Expansion   The United States

A Read a Chart

Look at The United States chart.

The United States		country	state	city
national anthem	The Star Spangled Banner by Francis Scott Key September 14th, 1814 0! say can you see by the dawn's early light,	X		
governor			X	
monument		X	X	X
city council				X
Supreme Court		X		

B Discuss

Talk about the chart. Take turns.

The state has a <u>governor</u>.

The country has a <u>national anthem</u>.

The city has a <u>monument</u> and a _____.

The country has a _____ and a <u>Supreme Court</u>.

The _____ has a _____.

C Make a Chart

Complete the chart in your notebook.

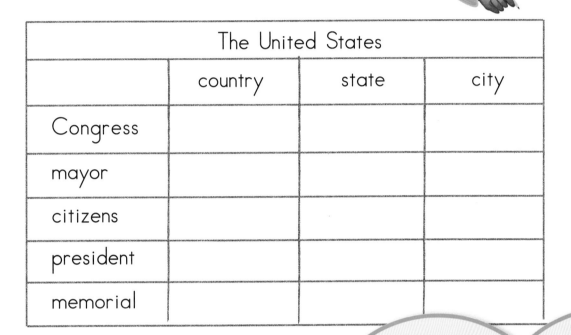

The United States			
	country	state	city
Congress			
mayor			
citizens			
president			
memorial			

D Discuss

Ask and answer questions about your chart. Take turns.

A: Does the city have <u>citizens</u>?

B: Yes, it has <u>citizens</u>.

B: Does the state have a <u>mayor</u>?

A: No, it doesn't have a <u>mayor</u>.

A: Does the _____ have _____?

B: Yes, it has _____.

B: Does the _____ have _____?

A: No, it doesn't have _____.

E Think Critically

Talk with your class.

List. Look at the charts.

1. What people and things does the country have?

2. What people and things does the city have?

Compare. Look at the charts.

1. How are the country, state, and city the same?

2. How are they different?

1. wash hands

2. exercise

3. drink water

4. sleep

5. floss

6. go to the dentist

7. get a checkup

8. cover mouth

9. use a tissue

10. wear sunblock

Describe Frequency

Use the adjective *every* to talk about how often people do things.

Elena flosses <u>every</u> day.
She gets a checkup <u>every</u> year.
She drinks water <u>every</u> day.
She uses a tissue <u>every</u> time she sneezes.

Talk about Elena's healthy habits.

Elena sleeps _____ day.
She covers her mouth _____ time she coughs.
She exercises _____.
She _____ every day.
She _____ every year.
She _____ every _____.

Smiling Faces!

 1. forehead

 4. nose

 7. tongue

 2. eyebrow

 5. mouth

 8. lips

 3. eyelid

 6. gums

 9. teeth

Silly Faces

Describe Faces

10. cheek

11. chin

12. ear

 Use the prepositions *above* and *below* to talk about faces.

The nose is <u>above</u> the mouth.
The chin is <u>below</u> the forehead.
The eyebrows are <u>above</u> the eyes.

Talk about faces.

The chin is _____ the nose.
The eyes are _____ the mouth.
The _____ is above the _____.
The _____ is below the _____.

95

39 Parts of the Body

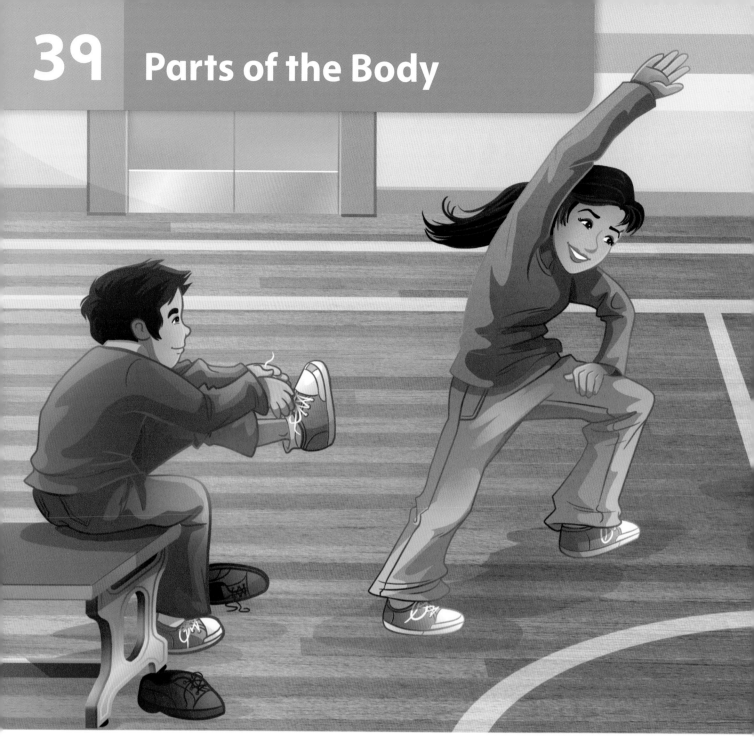

 1. head

 2. neck

 3. shoulder

 4. chest

 5. back

 6. leg

 7. knee

 8. foot

 9. ankle

 10. arm

 11. hand

 12. wrist

Describe Parts of the Body

Use the preposition *between* **to talk about the parts of the body.**

The wrist is <u>between</u> the hand and the arm.

The neck is <u>between</u> the head and the shoulders.

Talk about the parts of the body.

The _____ is between the foot and the leg.

The _____ is between the shoulders.

The _____ is between the _____.

40 More Parts of the Body

 1. brain

 2. heart

 3. lungs

 4. stomach

 5. muscle

 6. bone

 7. ribs

 8. skin

 9. finger

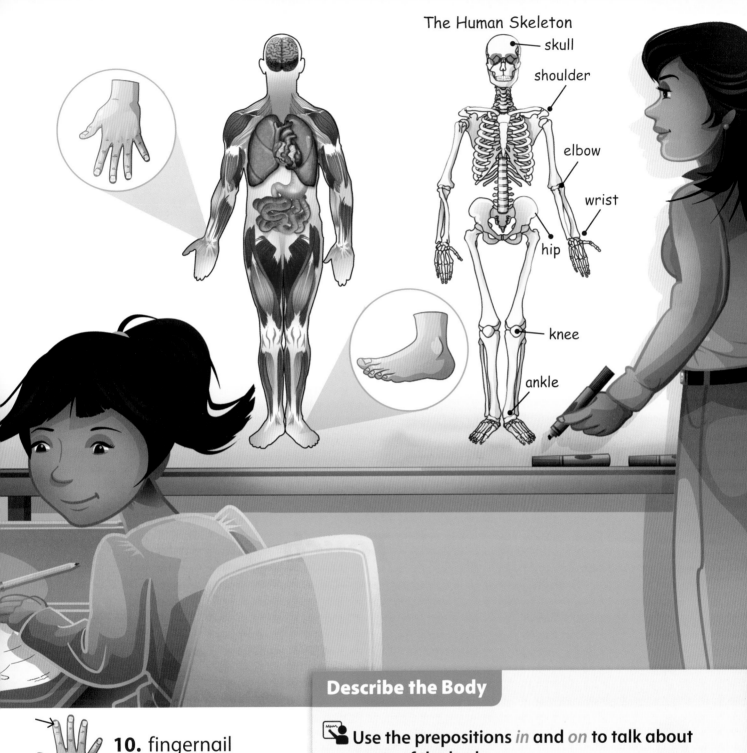

The Human Skeleton

- skull
- shoulder
- elbow
- wrist
- hip
- knee
- ankle

10. fingernail

11. toe

12. toenail

Describe the Body

Use the prepositions *in* and *on* to talk about parts of the body.

The heart is <u>in</u> the body.
Skin is <u>on</u> the body.
The brain is <u>in</u> the head.

Talk about parts of the body.

Toenails are on the _____.
_____ are in the body.
_____ is on the _____.
_____ is in the _____.

99

Sight

Touch

 1. see

 4. feel

 7. rough

 2. hear

 5. smell

 8. smooth

 3. taste

 6. shiny

 9. sweet

Taste

Quiet Please!

Hearing

Smell

10. sour

11. loud

12. quiet

Describe Senses

 Use adjectives to talk about people and senses.

She feels the <u>rough</u> rock.

He sees the <u>shiny</u> penny.

👥 Talk about people and senses.

She feels _____.

He hears _____.

She sees _____.

He smells _____.

She tastes _____.

42 Nutrition

 1. oatmeal

 4. peppers

 7. peach

 2. pasta

 5. sweet potato

 8. pear

 3. spinach

 6. corn

 9. yogurt

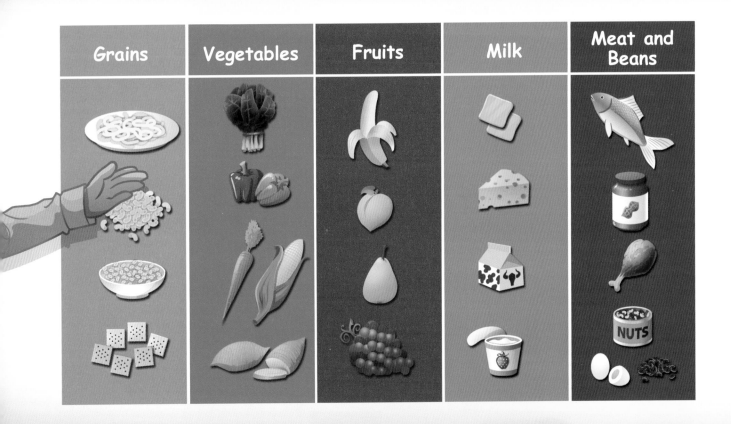

Grains	Vegetables	Fruits	Milk	Meat and Beans

Describe Food Groups

10. cheese

11. nuts

12. fish

 Use *part of* to talk about food groups.

A peach is <u>part of</u> the fruit group.
Pasta is <u>part of</u> the grain group.
Peppers are <u>part of</u> the vegetable group.
Nuts are <u>part of</u> the meat and bean group.

Talk about food groups.

Cheese is _____ the milk group.

_____ is part of the _____ group.

_____ are part of the _____ group.

103

A Read a Chart

Look at the Parts of the Body chart.

Parts of the Body

one	two	many
head	eyebrows	toes
neck	lips	fingernails
heart	lungs	bone

B Discuss

Talk about the chart. Take turns.

I have one <u>head</u>.

I have two <u>eyebrows</u>.

I have many _____.

I have _____.

C Make a Chart

Complete the chart in your notebook.

Word Box
back
brain
ears
knees
muscles
shoulders
stomach
teeth
toenails

Parts of the Body		
one	two	many

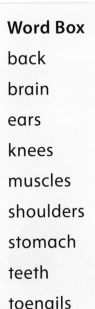

D Discuss

👥 **Ask and answer questions about your chart. Take turns.**

A: Do you have many <u>teeth</u>?

B: Yes, I have many <u>teeth</u>.

B: Do you have two <u>brains</u>?

A: No, I have one _____.

A: Do you have _____?

B: Yes, I have _____.

B: Do you have _____?

A: No, I have _____.

E Think Critically

👥 **Talk with your class.**

List. Look at the charts.

1. Name the body parts you have one of.

2. Name the body parts you have two of.

Infer. Look at the charts.

1. Do you have the same number of teeth and bones?

2. Is *many* a number you can count? Why or why not?

1. observe

2. magnifying glass

3. microscope

4. binoculars

5. measure

6. ruler

7. meter stick

8. measuring tape

9. measuring cup

10. thermometer

Discuss Science Processes

 Use *observe* and *measure* to talk about how to use science tools.

Use a magnifying glass to <u>observe</u>.
Use a meter stick to <u>measure</u>.
Use binoculars to <u>observe</u>.
Use a measuring cup to <u>measure</u>.

Talk about science tools.

Use a measuring tape to _____.
Use a microscope to _____.
Use a _____ to measure.
Use a _____ to observe.
Use a _____ to _____.

44 Plants

 1. flowers

 2. petal

 3. bud

 4. stem

 5. thorn

 6. leaf

 7. roots

 8. seeds

 9. seedling

Describe Plants

10. bulb

11. pollen

12. bee

👤 **Use the adjectives *small* and *large* to talk about plants.**

The tulip has <u>large</u> flowers.
The seedling has <u>small</u> roots.
The iris has <u>large</u> leaves.

👥 **Talk about the plants.**

The rose has _____ thorns.
The _____ has _____ petals.
The _____ has _____.

109

bison

kangaroo

tiger

 1. beak

 4. fur

 7. tail

 2. wing

 5. paw

 8. whiskers

 3. feather

 **6.** claw

 9. pouch

antelope

monkey

gorilla

10. antlers

11. hoof

12. shell

Discuss Animals

Use *Which* _____? to ask about animals.

A: <u>Which</u> animal has antlers?

B: The antelope has antlers.

B: <u>Which</u> animal has a tail?

A: The tiger has a tail.

Ask and answer questions about the animals.

A: Which animal has _____?

B: The _____ has _____.

111

46 Growing and Changing

 1. cocoon

 2. caterpillar

 3. butterfly

 4. tadpole

 5. frog

 6. kitten

 7. cat

 8. nest

 9. egg

Describe Change

10. chick

11. bird

12. hatch

Use the verb *becomes* to talk about how animals change.

The chick <u>becomes</u> a bird.
The tadpole <u>becomes</u> a frog.
The caterpillar <u>becomes</u> a butterfly.

Talk about how the animals change.

The kitten becomes a _____.
The cocoon becomes a _____.
The _____ becomes a _____.

 1. seaweed

 **4.** dolphin

 7. crab

 2. coral

 5. octopus

 8. fin

 3. shark

 6. ray

 9. gills

Describe Ocean Animals

10. scales

11. blowhole

12. tentacles

 Use the verb *has* to talk about animals and their body parts.

A dolphin <u>has</u> a blowhole.

A fish <u>has</u> scales.

An octopus <u>has</u> tentacles.

Talk about the animals.

A ray _____ gills.

A shark has _____.

A _____ has _____.

115

48　The Desert

 1. snake

 **4.** hawk

 7. rabbit

 **2.** lizard

 5. coyote

 8. mouse

 **3.** scorpion

 6. prairie dog

 9. cactus

10. sand

11. dunes

12. hole

Discuss Animal Behavior

Use *hides in* and *hides under* to talk about animals in the desert.

The bird <u>hides in</u> the cactus.
The scorpion <u>hides under</u> a rock.
The prairie dog <u>hides in</u> a hole.

Talk about where the animals hide.

The snake _____ a rock.
The mouse hides _____.
The _____ hides under _____.
The _____ hides in _____.

117

49 The Forest

 1. pine tree

 2. oak tree

 3. trunk

4. bark

 5. pine cone

 6. needles

 7. acorn

 8. bear

 9. deer

Discuss Similarities

10. squirrel

11. woodpecker

12. mosquito

🖍 **Use the adverb *too* to talk about how things are the same.**

A pine tree has a trunk.
An oak tree has a trunk <u>too</u>.

A deer has fur.
A bear has fur <u>too</u>.

👥 **Talk about the forest.**

A _____ has _____.
A _____ has _____ too.

50 The Rain Forest

 1. turtle

 **4.** owl

 7. moth

 2. jaguar

 5. parrot

 8. spider

 3. bat

 6. dragonfly

 9. ant

10. orchid

11. fern

12. moss

Describe Movement

🗣️ **Use the verbs *walks* and *flies* to talk about how animals move.**

A jaguar <u>walks</u>.
A moth <u>flies</u>.
A turtle <u>walks</u>.

👥 **Talk about how the animals move.**

An owl _____.
A _____ walks.
A _____ flies.

121

51 The Grassland

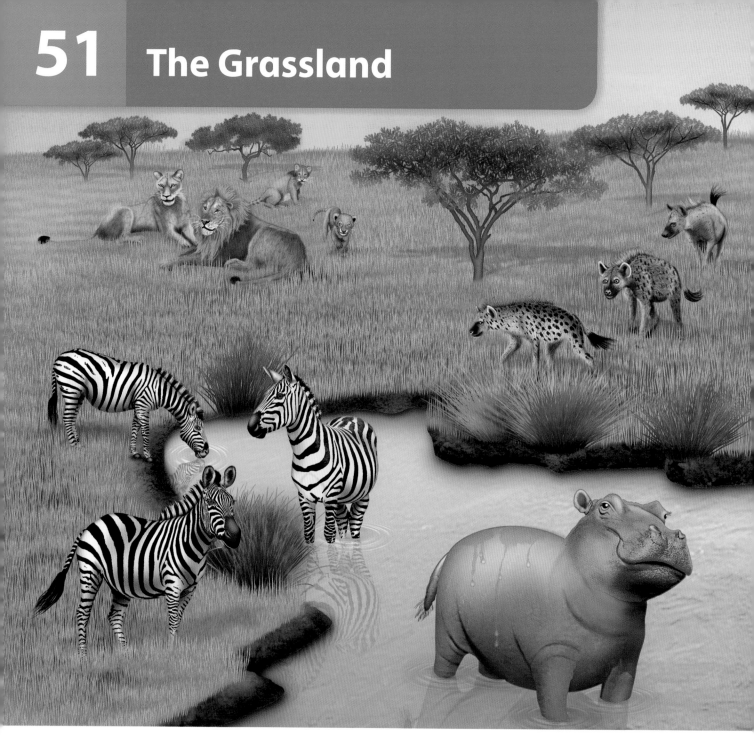

 1. watering hole

 2. grass

 3. flamingo

 4. lion

 **5.** hyena

 6. leopard

 7. hippopotamus

 8. zebra

 9. elephant

Determine Distance

10. giraffe

11. spots

12. stripes

Use the prepositions *near* and *far from* to talk about the animals.

The leopard is <u>far from</u> the giraffes.
The hippopotamus is <u>near</u> the zebras.
The lion is <u>far from</u> the watering hole.

Talk about the animals.

The flamingo is far from _____.
The _____ is near the trees.
The _____ is far from _____.
The _____ is near _____.

123

A Read a Chart

Look at the Animal Features chart.

Animal Features

		tail	wings	fin	paws
fish		X		X	
snake		X			
squirrel		X			X
parrot		X	X		
lion		X			X

B Discuss

Talk about the chart. Take turns.

A <u>parrot</u> has <u>wings</u>.

A <u>snake</u> has a <u>tail</u>.

A <u>lion</u> has a <u>tail</u> and _____.

A _____ has a <u>tail</u> and a <u>fin</u>.

A _____ has _____.

C Make a Chart

Complete the chart in your notebook.

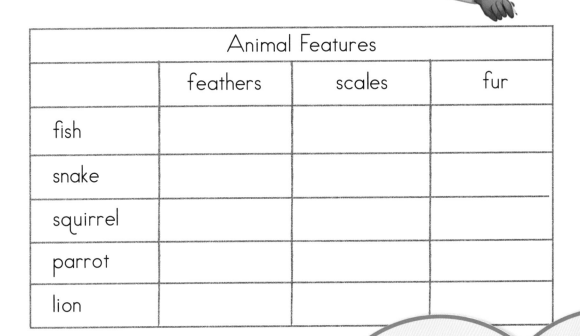

Animal Features			
	feathers	scales	fur
fish			
snake			
squirrel			
parrot			
lion			

D Discuss

Ask and answer questions about your chart. Take turns.

A: Does a <u>parrot</u> have <u>feathers</u>?

B: Yes, a <u>parrot</u> has <u>feathers</u>.

B: Does a <u>lion</u> have <u>scales</u>?

A: No, a <u>lion</u> doesn't have <u>scales</u>.

A: Does a _____ have _____?

B: Yes, a _____ has _____.

B: Does a _____ have _____?

A: No, a _____ doesn't have _____.

E Think Critically

Talk with your class.

List. Look at the charts.

1. How many animals have a tail? Name them.

2. How many animals have scales? Name them.

Compare. Look at the charts.

1. How are a fish and a snake the same?

2. Pick two other animals. How are they the same?

1. predict

2. test

3. pour

4. record

5. compare

6. graph

7. sort

8. diagram

9. chart

10. explain

Sequence Steps in a Process

 Use *first* and *then* to talk about steps in science.

<u>First</u>, predict.
<u>Then</u>, test.

<u>First</u>, pour water.
<u>Then</u>, record the amount.

<u>First</u>, make a chart.
<u>Then</u>, explain the chart.

👥 Talk about steps in science.

_____, sort objects.

_____, draw a diagram.

_____, compare weights.

_____, make a graph.

First, _____.
Then, _____.

 1. solid

 2. liquid

 3. gas

 4. wood

 5. metal

 6. ice

 7. mix

 8. sink

 9. float

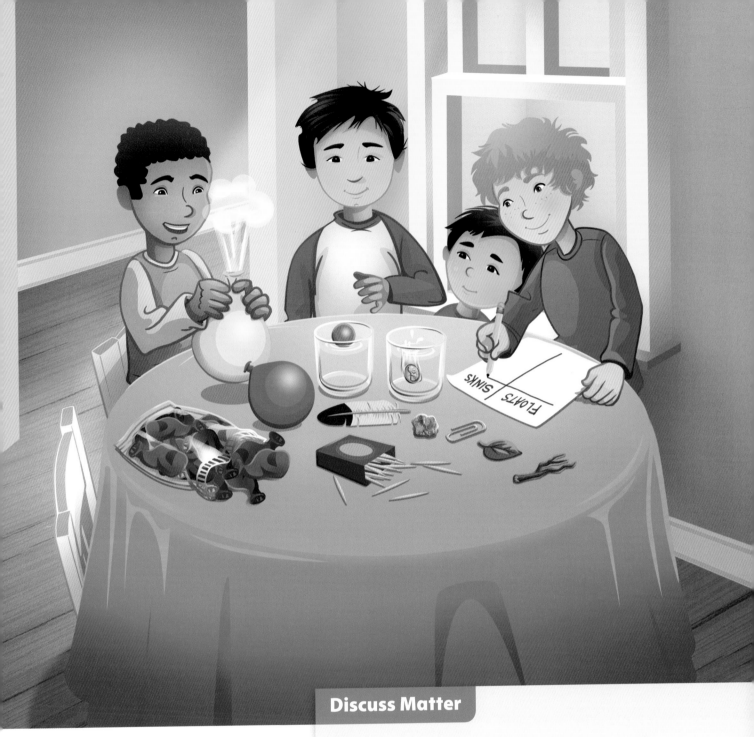

10. freeze

11. melt

12. boil

Discuss Matter

Use verbs to ask and answer questions about matter.

A: Does water <u>freeze</u>?

B: Yes, water <u>freezes</u>.

Ask and answer questions about matter.

A: Does ice melt?

B: Yes, ice _____.

B: Does _____?

A: _____.

 1. guitar

 4. piano

 7. iron

 2. drum

 5. oven

 8. candle

 3. whistle

 6. grill

 9. prism

OXFORD CRAFT FAIR

10. rainbow

11. reflection

12. shadow

Identify Sources

 Use *source of* to talk about heat, light, and sound.

The whistle is a <u>source of</u> sound.
The iron is a <u>source of</u> heat.
The candle is a <u>source of</u> light.

Talk about heat, light, and sound.

The oven is a _____ heat.
The lamp is a _____ light.
The _____ is a source of sound.
The _____ is a source of _____.

131

55 Motion and Force

 1. slide

 2. swing

 3. wheels

 4. magnet

 5. attract

 6. roll

 7. drop

 8. push

 **9.** pull

132 Unit 7 Physical Science

Describe Action

10. speed up

11. slow down

12. stop

📝 **Use a verb with *-ing* to talk about what someone or something is doing.**

The ball is <u>rolling</u>.
The girl is <u>going</u> down the slide.
The boy is <u>speeding</u> up.

👥 **Talk about what people and things are doing.**

The woman is _____ the swing.
The boy is _____ the wagon.
_____ is _____.

1. lawn mower

2. fan

3. flashlight

4. light bulb

5. wire

6. cord

7. plug

8. outlet

9. light switch

Identify Energy Sources

 10. gas

 11. battery

 12. electricity

Use *runs on* to talk about things that use energy.

The fan <u>runs on</u> electricity.
The flashlight <u>runs on</u> batteries.
The lawn mower <u>runs on</u> gas.

Talk about things that use energy.

The toy dog _____ batteries.
The lamp runs on _____.
The _____ runs on _____.

135

A Read a Chart

Look at the Sources of Energy chart.

Sources of Energy			
	heat	light	sound
light bulb		X	
guitar			X
iron	X		
candle	X	X	
flashlight		X	

B Discuss

Talk about the chart. Take turns.

A <u>light bulb</u> is a source of light.

A <u>candle</u> is a source of heat and light.

A <u>guitar</u> is a source of _____.

A _____ is a source of _____.

C Make a Chart

Complete the chart in your notebook.

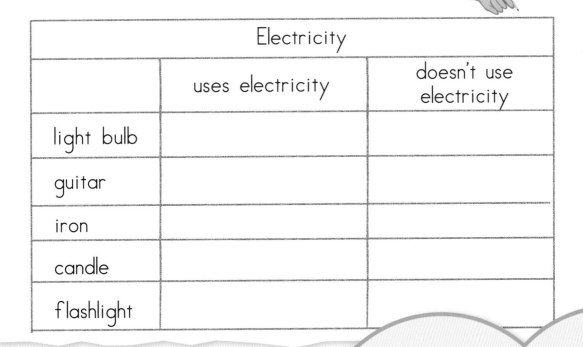

Electricity		
	uses electricity	doesn't use electricity
light bulb		
guitar		
iron		
candle		
flashlight		

D Discuss

Ask and answer questions about your chart. Take turns.

A: Does an <u>iron</u> use electricity?

B: Yes, it uses electricity.

B: Does a <u>candle</u> use electricity?

A: No, it doesn't use electricity.

A: Does a _____ use electricity?

B: Yes, _____.

B: Does a _____ use electricity?

A: No, _____.

E Think Critically

Talk with your class.

List. Look at the charts.

1. What is a source of light?

2. What uses electricity?

Make Connections. Look at the charts.

1. Which things use electricity and give light?

2. What other things do you know that use electricity?

137

1. mountain

2. volcano

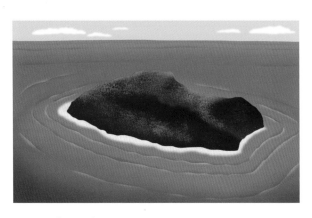

3. island

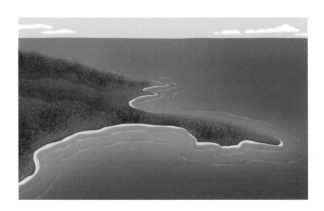

4. peninsula

5. bay

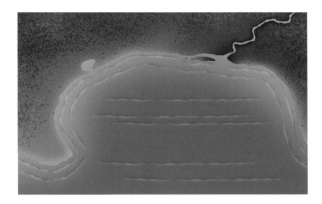

6. gulf

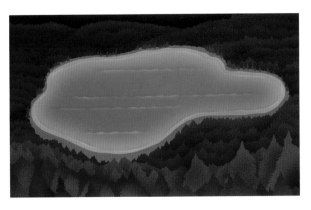

7. lake

8. plain

9. plateau

10. canyon

📝 **Use the conjunction *or* to ask questions about landforms and bodies of water.**

A: Is a bay a landform <u>or</u> a body of water?

B: It's a body of water.

B: Is an island a landform <u>or</u> a body of water?

A: It's a landform.

👥 **Ask and answer questions about landforms and bodies of water.**

A: Is a plain a landform or a body of water?

B: It's a _____.

B: Is a _____ a landform or a body of water?

A: It's a _____.

 1. mountain range

 4. hill

 7. dam

 2. glacier

 5. valley

 8. cave

 3. cliff

 6. waterfall

 9. steep

Describe the Landforms

 10. level

 11. high

 12. low

 Use adjectives **to talk about the landforms.**

The mountain range is <u>high</u>.
The valley is <u>low</u>.
The plain is <u>level</u>.

Talk about the landforms.

The _____ is steep.
The waterfall is _____.
The _____ is _____.

141

59 Earth Materials

 1. rocks

 4. crystal

 7. clay

 2. pebble

 5. soil

 8. lava

 3. boulder

 6. mud

 9. models

EROSION

WEATHERING

Describe Earth Materials

 10. layer

 11. hard

 12. soft

Use adjectives to talk about earth materials.

The crystal is <u>hard</u>.

The clay is <u>soft</u>.

The boulder is <u>large</u>.

The pebble is <u>small</u>.

Talk about earth materials.

The _____ is soft.

The _____ is hard.

The _____ is _____.

143

60 Dinosaurs and Fossils

Tyrannosaurus rex

Stegosaurus

 1. dinosaurs

 4. horn

 7. fossil

 2. skeleton

 5. spike

 8. plant-eater

 3. skull

 6. footprint

 9. meat-eater

Diplodocus

Triceratops

Describe Dinosaurs

10. scientist

11. sharp

12. flat

 Use the verb *had* to talk about dinosaurs.

Triceratops <u>had</u> horns.
Plant-eaters <u>had</u> flat teeth.
Tyrannosaurus rex <u>had</u> sharp teeth.

👥 **Talk about the dinosaurs.**

Tyrannosaurus rex _____ a large skull.
Meat-eaters had _____ teeth.
Stegosaurus had _____.
_____ had _____.

145

61 Weather

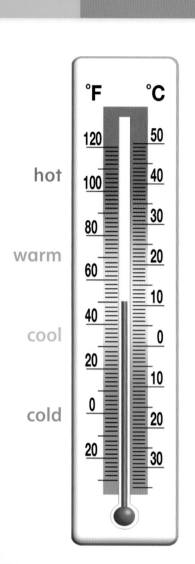

hot

warm

cool

cold

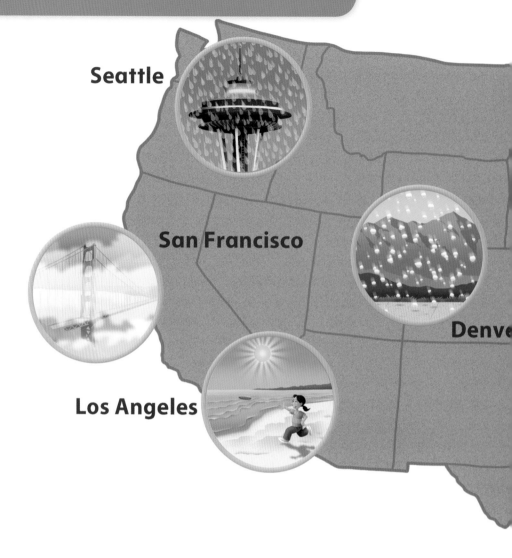

Seattle

San Francisco

Los Angeles

Denve

 1. temperature

 4. snow

 7. fog

 2. sunshine

 5. hail

 8. lightning

 3. rain

 6. wind

 9. thunderstorm

Minneapolis

New York

St. Louis

Oklahoma City

Dallas

Miami

10. hurricane

11. tornado

12. blizzard

Use the verb *was* to talk about yesterday's weather.

There <u>was</u> fog in San Francisco.

There <u>was</u> rain in Seattle.

There <u>was</u> a blizzard in Minneapolis.

Talk about the weather.

There was _____ in Dallas.

There was _____ in New York.

There was _____ in _____.

147

 1. wave

 2. river

 3. stream

 4. pond

 5. salt water

 6. fresh water

 7. vapor

 8. cloud

 9. drops

Water Cycle

Discuss Water

10. evaporation

11. condensation

12. precipitation

Use the adverb *also* to talk about water.

A river has fresh water.
A pond <u>also</u> has fresh water.

Evaporation is part of the water cycle.
Condensation is <u>also</u> part of the water cycle.

Talk about water.

Vapor is part of the water cycle.
_____ is <u>also</u> part of the water cycle.

149

63 The Environment

 1. pollution

 4. litter

 7. glass

 2. smog

 5. garbage

 8. plastic

 3. exhaust

 6. cardboard

 9. aluminum

10. bins

11. recycle

12. throw away

Describe Action

Use a verb with *-ing* to talk about what someone is doing.

She is <u>picking</u> up litter.

He is <u>recycling</u> cardboard.

She is <u>throwing</u> away trash.

Talk about what the people are doing.

He is _____ the plastic.

She is _____ the glass.

_____ is _____.

151

Sun

Mercury

Venus

Earth

Mars

Jupiter

 1. solar system

 4. orbit

 7. star

 2. planets

 5. moon phases

 8. constellation

 3. moon

 6. ring

 9. comet

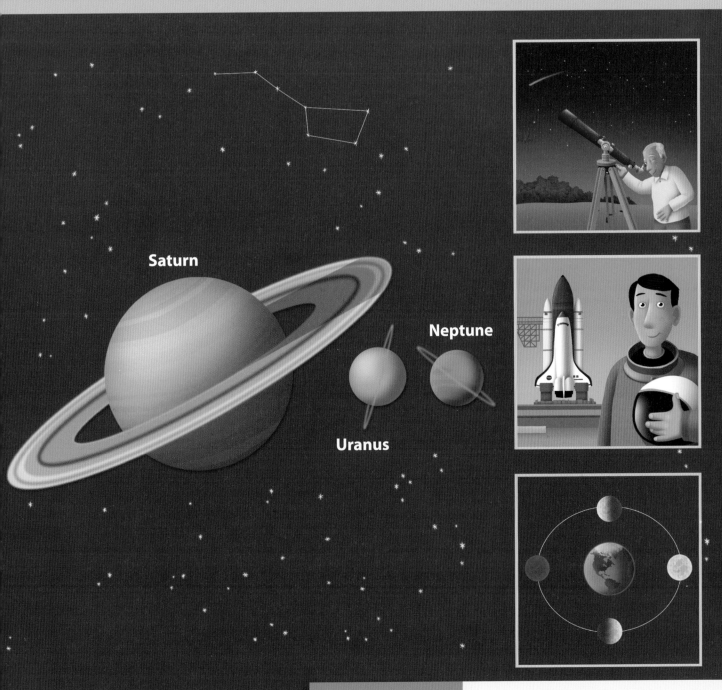

Saturn

Neptune

Uranus

Discuss Space

10. telescope

11. rocket

12. astronaut

 Use *What is* _____? **to ask questions about space.**

A: <u>What is</u> Mercury?

B: Mercury is a planet.

B: <u>What is</u> a constellation?

A: A constellation is a group of stars.

Ask and answer questions about space.

A: What is _____?

B: _____.

A Read a Diagram

Look at the Earth Features diagram.

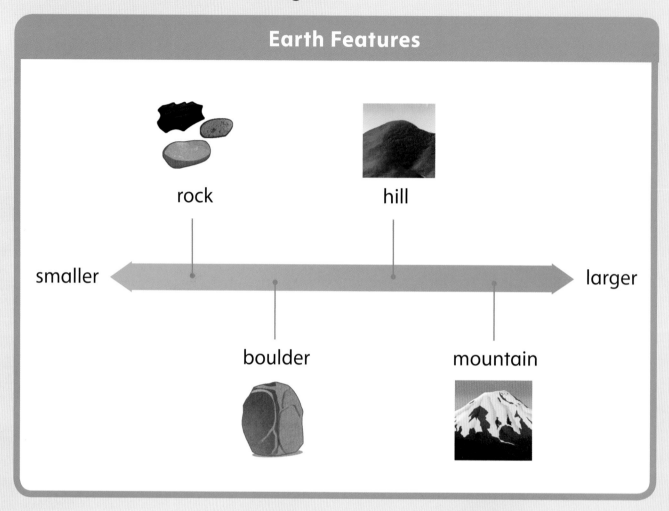

Earth Features

rock   hill

smaller ————————————————————————→ larger

boulder   mountain

B Discuss

👥 **Talk about the diagram. Take turns.**

A <u>boulder</u> is smaller than a <u>hill</u>.

A <u>mountain</u> is larger than a <u>rock</u>.

A <u>hill</u> is smaller than a _____.

A _____ is larger than a _____.

A _____ is _____ than a _____.

C Make a Diagram

Complete the diagram in your notebook.

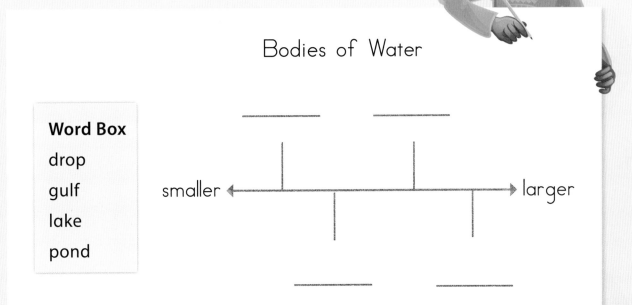

Bodies of Water

Word Box

drop

gulf

lake

pond

smaller ← → larger

D Discuss

Ask and answer questions about your diagram. Take turns.

A: Is a <u>lake</u> smaller than a <u>gulf</u>?

B: Yes, a <u>lake</u> is smaller than a <u>gulf</u>.

B: Is a <u>pond</u> larger than a <u>lake</u>?

A: No, a <u>pond</u> isn't larger than a <u>lake</u>.

A: Is a _____ smaller than a _____?

B: _____.

B: Is a _____ larger than a _____?

A: _____.

E Think Critically

Talk with your class.

Identify. Look at the diagrams.

1. What is the smallest earth feature?

2. What is the largest body of water?

Make Connections. Look at the diagrams.

1. What is smaller than a rock?

2. What is larger than a gulf?

1. five o'clock

2. five fifteen

3. five thirty

4. five forty-five

5. hour hand

6. minute hand

7. hour

8. minute

9. a.m.

10. p.m.

Determine Time

Use the preposition *on* to talk about the hands on the clock.

A: The hour hand is <u>on</u> the 5.
The minute hand is <u>on</u> the 12.
What time is it?

B: It's 5:00.

B: The hour hand is <u>on</u> the 5.
The minute hand is <u>on</u> the 9.
What time is it?

A: It's 5:45.

Talk about the clock.

A: The hour hand is _____ the 5.
The minute hand is _____ the 3.
What time is it?

B: It's 5:15.

B: The hour hand is on the _____.
The minute hand is on the _____.
What time is it?

A: It's _____.

2+3=5 **1.** problem

 4. multiply

 **7.** even numbers

+ **2.** add

÷ **5.** divide

8. odd numbers

— **3.** subtract

= **6.** equals

0 1 2 3 4 **9.** number line

Read Math Problems

> **10.** greater than

< **11.** less than

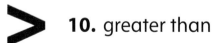 **12.** count

 Use these words to read math symbols.

+	2 + 3	two <u>plus</u> three
–	5 – 2	five <u>minus</u> two
×	2 × 3	two <u>times</u> three
÷	6 ÷ 2	six <u>divided by</u> two
=	2 + 3 = 5	two plus three <u>equals</u> five

 Use symbols to make math problems. Then read.

5 _____ 3 = _____

6 _____ 3 = _____

159

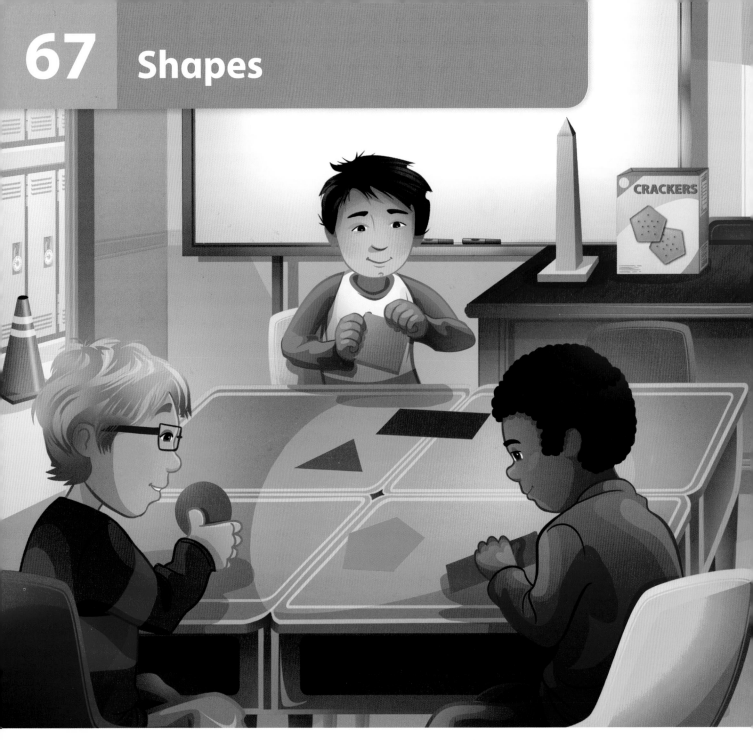

 1. circle

 4. rectangle

 7. pyramid

 2. triangle

 5. pentagon

 8. cube

 3. square

 6. sphere

 9. cylinder

Describe Shapes

10. cone

11. side

12. angle

 Use numbers to talk about shapes.

A triangle has <u>three</u> sides.
A square has <u>four</u> angles.
A pentagon has <u>five</u> sides.

Talk about shapes.

A rectangle has _____ angles.
A _____ has _____ sides.
A _____ has _____ angles.

A _____ has _____.

161

PLACE VALUE

3.1

3.14

3.141

2 3 5

	1. whole		**4.** one fourth	→$\frac{1}{4}$	**7.** numerator
	2. one half	**1,2,3**	**5.** whole numbers	→$\frac{1}{4}$	**8.** denominator
	3. one third	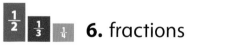	**6.** fractions		**9.** equal parts

WHOLE 1.0	1			
HALF 0.5	$\frac{1}{2}$		$\frac{1}{2}$	
THIRD 0.33	$\frac{1}{3}$	$\frac{1}{3}$	$\frac{1}{3}$	
FOURTH 0.25	$\frac{1}{4}$	$\frac{1}{4}$	$\frac{1}{4}$	$\frac{1}{4}$

$$\frac{\frac{1}{4}}{\frac{1}{4}} = \frac{1}{2}$$

$$\frac{2}{4} = \frac{1}{2}$$

0.25 **10.** decimal point
↑

0.25 **11.** tenths place
↑

0.25 **12.** hundredths place
↑

Discuss Fractions

Use *does* and *doesn't* to ask and answer questions about fractions.

A: <u>Does</u> he have one whole circle?

B: Yes, he <u>does</u>.

B: <u>Does</u> she have one fourth of a circle?

A: No, she <u>doesn't</u>. She has one third of a circle.

Ask and answer questions about fractions.

A: Does _____ have _____?

B: _____.

163

 1. inch

 4. centimeter

 7. pint

 2. foot

 5. meter

 8. quart

 3. yard

 6. cup

 9. gallon

10. liter

11. ounce

12. gram

Compare Units of Measure

Use adjectives with *–er* to talk about units of measure.

A meter is <u>longer</u> than a centimeter.
A gallon is <u>larger</u> than a cup.
Five ounces is <u>heavier</u> than one ounce.

Talk about units of measure.

A pint is _____ than a quart.
An inch is _____ than a _____.
_____ is _____ than a _____.

1, 2, 3…

MONEY	VALUE
	1¢
	5¢
	10¢
	25¢
	100¢

 1. penny

 2. nickel

 3. dime

4. quarter

 5. dollar

1¢ **6.** cent

 7. coins

 8. bills

 9. price

Discuss Value

10. buy

11. sell

12. save

Use *How much _____?* to ask about money.

A: <u>How much</u> is a nickel worth?

B: A nickel is worth 5 cents.

B: <u>How much</u> is a quarter worth?

A: A quarter is worth 25 cents.

Ask and answer questions about money.

A: How much is a _____ worth?

B: A _____ is worth _____.

167

A Read a Diagram

Look at the Fractions diagram.

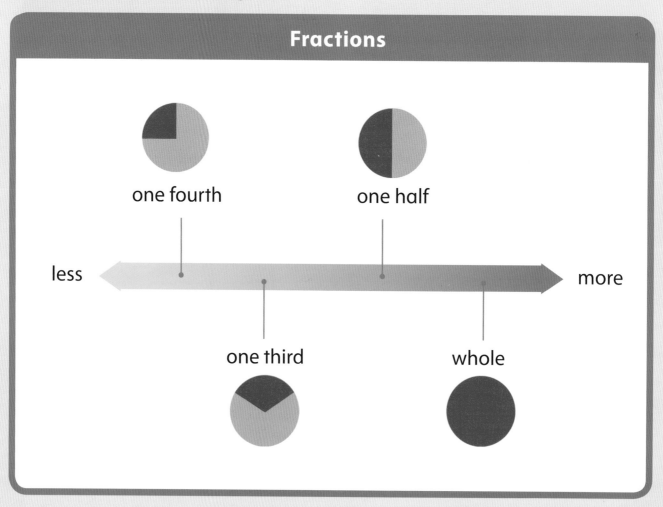

Fractions

one fourth

one half

less   more

one third

whole

B Discuss

Talk about the diagram. Take turns.

One half is more than one third.

One fourth is less than one half.

One whole is more than _____.

_____ is less than _____.

_____ is _____ than _____.

C Make a Diagram

Complete the diagram in your notebook.

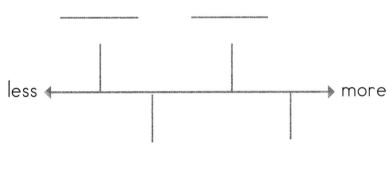

Liquid Measures

Word Box
cup
gallon
pint
quart

less ←————————————→ more

D Discuss

👥 **Ask and answer questions about your diagram. Take turns.**

A: Is a <u>quart</u> more than a <u>cup</u>?

B: Yes, it is more than a <u>cup</u>.

B: Is a <u>gallon</u> less than a <u>pint</u>?

A: No, it isn't less than a <u>pint</u>.

A: Is a _____ more than a _____?

B: _____.

B: Is a _____ less than a _____?

A: _____.

E Think Critically

👥 **Talk with your class.**

Apply. Look at both diagrams.
1. What is the smallest fraction?

2. What is the largest liquid measure?

Make Connections. Look at both diagrams.
1. When do you use fractions and liquid measures together?

2. How else do you use fractions?

169

Index

The number(s) to the right of each entry tell the page(s) the words are on. Page numbers in pink show labels from the pictures.